TURNING MONKEYS INTO LEMONS

Lee Gilbert

Published 2008 by arima publishing

www.arimapublishing.com

ISBN 978-1-84549-299-1

Printed and bound in the United Kingdom

Typeset in Verdana

arima publishing
ASK House, Northgate Avenue
Bury St Edmunds, Suffolk IP32 6BB
t: (+44) 01284 700321

www.arimapublishing.com

Acknowledgements

I want to say thank you to everyone who has contributed to my being able to write this book, to the people I have met, and to the other coaches, consultants, teachers and trainers whom I have learned from over a 10 year period. Maybe more so, I would like to acknowledge all the people I have trained and coached in this period – you have provided me with tremendous experience and great quantities of quotable and teachable examples to pass on. Although I'm often sat on the "experts" side of the table – I've learned and taken great stories from many clients and the people I've met.

To those that feel that life is a journey, you're wrong – life is an endless lesson...

About the Author

Lee Gilbert is a successful Consultant, Trainer and Coach with over 10 years of experience.

He works internationally designing and delivering measurable Management Training and People Development solutions for organisations wanting to transform their culture, results and people. He believes in the principle of "Teaching" - the concept of developing others through memorable lessons. All of his work is based on his personal experience and he has a pragmatic view - preferring commercial conversations to theoretical ones - often challenging people that talk concept and cannot translate into reality.

His areas of specialism include: Management Training, Leadership Training, Performance Management, Culture Change, SMART Objective Setting, Coaching, Appraisal Skills Competency Frameworks, Communication Skills and Team Building.

Lee Gilbert is regarded as one of the leading Trainers, Consultants and Coaches in the UK - to make contact with him directly, visit his website: www.leegilbert.co.uk

Contents

Introduction

FOR EVERY MONKEY THERE ARE TWO PARTIES INVOLVED: ONE TO WORK IT AND ONE TO SUPERVISE IT
... William Oncken, Jr.

Turning Monkeys Into Lemons is doubtless a puzzling title. "Where is he going with that," you might be asking yourself. Now that I have your attention ... I'll tell you that this is a management book – a practical guide for managers and leaders on managing performance from an adult perspective, empowering and inspiring your team to take responsibility, and refocusing your self-management to create more discretionary time so you are able to channel your energy into leading your people rather than continuously taking on their work problems.

This mixed metaphor was chosen to point out the vast difference between managers who shoulder other people's problems and those who lead their people with enthusiasm, confidence and high-energy, inspiring their people to behave the same way. The concepts presented in this book are derived from two distinctive theories. First, that both managers and employees tend to replicate the parent-child relationship in the business environment. Second, that managers who get caught up in behaviours that encourage their employees to bring all problems to the "boss" for resolution reduce their effectiveness, disempower their employees, and find most of their office time consumed by problem-solving. Managers who feel forced to concentrate on issuing orders, directing activities, and taking on their direct reports' problems have no time to coach them into becoming more self-reliant and productive, more energetic and enthusiastic, and more willing to commit themselves to achieving personal and business objectives. *Turning Monkeys Into*

> **Managing performance from an Adult perspective is about empowering and inspiring your team to take responsibility.**

1

Lemons will help managers and leaders take time management wisdom and apply it with a pragmatic and practical approach to dealing with employees as adults who are energised by effective coaching, rather than children who can't be trusted to make responsible decisions.

If you even question whether this book will benefit you, answer the following questions:

1. How many times have you looked at your desk and wanted to set a match to it because you know you can't possibly get through everything within your business deadlines?

2. How many times a day do your direct reports pop into your office or stop you in the corridor to ask a "quick" question, and then leave an hour later, after which, you add another item to your to-do list?

3. How often do you dread a pending confrontation with a "difficult" employee ... one you feel behaves immaturely?

4. How frequently do you hear direct reports grumbling because you have vetoed another plan, proposal or programme after they presented you with what they felt was a brilliant idea?

5. How often do you wonder why you constantly have to look over your direct reports' shoulders and keep them from getting into trouble because of their poor decision-making?

6. How many times are you the last one out of the office at night ... wondering as you walk to your car why you seem to be the only one who is dedicated enough to face their responsibilities? ... And wondering why you are the only one who has no life?

If you answered anything besides "rarely" to any of these questions, you need this book because you are caught up in both the Monkey Syndrome[1] and a pattern of leadership that defines you as the critical parent and your employees as the adaptive children.[2]

Managers and leaders who are perpetually frustrated by their direct reports' seeming inability to make good decisions, who frequently wonder why they have to solve every problem themselves, and who are fed up with employees who whine and moan about their responsibilities or agree with the direction you set and then do as they please, may have unconsciously fallen into patterns of management that defeat their efforts to build effective teams who are ready for action, willing to learn and motivated to give their best. What managers who feel these frustrations often say to me is that they are sick of dealing with the problems their direct reports are unable to solve. Some describe a situation in which their direct report demonstrates a lack of decision-making capability by dumping every problem on their manager's desk, without attempting to think through alternative ways to handle it, or better yet, taking care of the problem themselves because it is their responsibility, before their manager has to deal with it. Often, though, those same managers also want to approve every decision before it is carried out, thereby reinforcing for their direct reports the notion that their manager doesn't trust them to make the right decisions and forcing them into the position of supplicant — asking permission and seeking approval. What does that remind you of? It reminds me of a child who goes to his parents each time to ask permission to watch the telly, rather than knowing the rules of the house and abiding by them independently, thus proving his trustworthiness and self-reliance.

---

1   William Oncken, "Managing Management Time: Who's Got The Monkey," *Harvard Business Review* (November 1974)

2   Eric Berne, "Games People Play: Basic Handbook of Transactional Analysis," Ballantine Books, 1996

While business circumstances frequently bring out the worst in people, a controlling and judgmental management style that reinforces childish behaviours only perpetuates the cycle of parent–child interaction. None of us feels comfortable thinking of ourselves as behaving childishly in business — certainly; it's not something we get up each morning deciding to do. It occurs because of the cause and effect relationship in our interpersonal transactions. Here's an example:

> You, as the new manager of an established department, are dealing with a multitude of issues, all of which require your attention. At the same time, you don't know your staff, and have only the assessment of the previous manager on which to base your decisions. If the impressions given you by the previous manager leave you with questions about the maturity and capabilities of your staff, all of whom are unknown to you, you may decide that you will want to personally approve every decision in order to make sure that operations continue to run smoothly as you acquaint yourself with your staff and their individual capabilities.

> On the other hand, your new employees have a history with the previous manager. Imagine that they are hoping their new manager will come in with enthusiasm and energy, sparking new ideas and new ways of thinking and giving them the freedom to pursue their own good ideas for improving departmental operations. At the very least, they assume they will be able to operate independently within the parameters of their positions. Anticipating an opportunity to really shine in front of a new boss and to become more effective in their jobs by "stepping up to the plate" and taking responsibility, your employees proceed as though their previous track records are proven and unblemished, you trust them to do their jobs, and you are ready to let them take the lead.

> What happens is a total disconnect between what <u>you</u> are thinking and what <u>they</u> are thinking about the situation. They are ready to move forward full steam ahead, while you are not ready to let them make decisions without your approval. So when they eagerly attempt to impress you with their actions, you feel horrified when they "jump the gun" and

take action without your approval, you reprimand them in one way or another, and then set up the requirement that they pass all decisions and potential actions by you for approval before doing anything. See where this is going? The employees' efforts to behave in a way they feel is empowered and responsible result in the manager reacting as a frustrated parent, which elicits resentment and childish reactions from employees, which further proves the manager's point that employees are behaving childishly and can't be trusted ... and the vicious cycle continues.

It will be difficult for employees to pull themselves out of this downward spiral into childhood. They will react negatively to what they perceive as unjust criticism and a blatant withholding of trust. The manager, on the other hand, will have a hard time building up trust with direct reports who appear to be behaving as he was warned they would. From his perspective, these people are continuing a pattern of taking risky action without confirming that their actions are correct. And at this point in the manager's process of adjustment to a new position and new employees, he may not be able to make a clear judgment about what is risky because of a lack of historical information about the company, department and situation ... history that could be supplied by his employees if they could be trusted to present a clear and insightful perspective. This situation is reminiscent of many that are familiar to parents of children who are mentally ready to make their own decisions, but still too emotionally immature to discern more objective and effective methods.

Contrasted against the organisation driven by the Monkey Syndrome, characterised by demotivated, frustrated, stressed-out people, is the Lemon organisation. That is one in which managers, leaders and employees at all levels face their work with zest: energy, enthusiasm, confidence, a willingness to learn, readiness for action and a positive approach to their work and the environment in which they do it.

> **A Lemon organisation is full of ZEST ... people with energy, enthusiasm, confidence, a willingness to learn, readiness for action and a positive approach to the work they do.**

Lemon managers are able to create discretionary time for themselves, and seldom, if ever, get caught up in managing a direct report's Monkey. They feel empowered themselves because they are the right people in the right job, so they are prepared to create an environment of empowerment for their people. They are leaders as well as managers; these high-performing individuals see opportunity around those who report to them and they make coaching and a certain kind of 'teaching' ... in more of a Zen context than a traditional instructional teaching perspective ... an integral part of the way they conduct business. In other words, they are able to foster an atmosphere of continuous learning wherein their direct reports can bring out the best, and the zest, in themselves.

As Lemon managers succeed, they are leading by example, because of their abilities to approach their own organisation-imposed and boss-imposed responsibilities with intelligence, wit and commitment. They operate in their Adult mode, using appropriate language and behaviours that provide a model for their direct reports. In modeling their own Lemon behaviours and strengths, these managers lead by example, encouraging their people to own their initiative and get out of the Monkey-passing paradigm. Individuals who learn to do this become Lemons themselves, which ups the ante for the whole team/department. Their zest and Lemon behaviour takes up less of their Manager's time and energy ... they are able to fend for themselves, and in fact they thrive on being capable and confident, knowing they are fully prepared and feeling completely empowered to handle their responsibilities. Put together, the combination of Lemon managers and Lemon direct reports make powerful, productive self-actualising teams — and they succeed in meeting established objectives, collectively and individually.

At the same time, Lemon managers are thriving on the leadership capabilities they have built within themselves, using their skill sets, their self-knowledge and their understanding, to maintain a sense of inner drive and confidence, regardless of what befalls the organisation. Even Lemon organisations face external hardship, but they are set up to win because their people have the built-in drive and flexibility to handle what the business world throws at them.

The thing I have found particularly inspiring about Lemon organisations is that they know who they are. They have a clearly defined set of values, that are shared by the majority of leaders, managers and employees. They actually live their values, and it shows in the organisation's flexibility, ability to withstand cyclical economic downturns or global crises. In turn, their people know who they are as well. Employees of a Lemon company, at all levels, know why they work for that company, as well as what they get out of it, and that it resides mentally at a higher level than pay and benefits; because in the end, pay is really not a great motivator. Oh, it may be motivating for about a week after a raise is given, but after that it becomes the norm again ... the baseline measure that everything else is built upon. Fulfilment comes at a much deeper level, and I've found that the leaders of Lemon organisations understand this. They know that the high-producing workforce is engaged and **producing** because they are there for more than the salary and bonuses they receive, and that they receive more than just pay: they receive the challenge of work that inspires and fulfils them, they feel trust and mutual respect from superiors and colleagues, and they are motivated to contribute to the achievement of the objectives of the organisation.

> **A high-performing team is engaged and producing because they are there for more than the paycheck they receive.**

One objective of this book is to look at ways to change from Monkey-driven behaviour to more Lemon-like behaviour. As illustrated in one of the Lessons Learned from Chapter Two, one business owner I worked with had to physically take time off from his own business to learn the lessons of Parental-mode Monkey management, but learn he did. He came to realise that not only could he trust his employees to do the right thing, but that they would also do the right thing with more ease and finesse when he wasn't around. His own behaviour was stunting their growth and inhibiting their abilities to take control of their own responsibilities. Much of what we cover is about changing behaviours, many of which are unconscious and unintentional. What it takes is a figurative 'hit over the head' to shock managers awake to the consequences of their own actions.

ally just human nature. What we have done for so long we often take for
and assume that it works until something is thrown in our path that
home the point that it's **not** working.

In addition to defining and highlighting the positive and negative behaviours
exemplified by the Monkey Syndrome and Lemon organisations, *Turing Monkeys
Into Lemons* puts into sharp relief against those concepts the traditional issues of
performance management, performance appraisal, absence management,
succession planning, competencies and objective setting, giving and getting
feedback, communication and managing difficult people. These are all
challenging enough to handle for any manager, but saddled with Monkeys, it is
terribly daunting. What this book is about is
uncovering ways that Lemon behaviour will create
energies and synergies within a company,
department and team that help managers make
sense of those traditional management activities.

**Managers living the
Monkey Syndrome fall
victim to helping
create unmeasurable
objectives that fail to
help the subordinate
stretch and reach
meaningful, fulfilling
goals.**

What happens when a manager, overwhelmed with
taking charge and controlling the decisions and
outcomes for countless employees, is faced with
high absenteeism, a low-performing team and
ineffective direct reports? This person is sinking
under the weight of Monkeys without a life
preserver. His first error lies in not trusting his
people to manage their own work or projects, in taking on their "Monkeys" and in
controlling them through the Parental Tell and Do attitude. Not only has he lost
his discretionary time to handle his own areas of responsibility that are
organisationally-driven or boss-driven; he hasn't a hope of effectively addressing
the causes of the absenteeism and poor performance. He can't see that it is the
environment of disempowerment that he is creating that is responsible for much
of these issues; and he has no idea how to communicate with his direct reports
in an open, Adult fashion, so he will never be able to figure it out without
intervention.

Managing performance is so much more than dutifully conducting reviews according to schedule. These managers fall victim to helping create immeasurable objectives that fail to help the direct report stretch and reach meaningful or fulfilling objectives. Frequently, they approach the entire performance management process as a dreaded responsibility to be gotten out of the way as quickly as possible, rather than recognising it for the great opportunity to coach and teach their direct reports. Growing employees into Lemons requires the fertilising nutrients of encouragement, confidence building and belief in the employee's ability to succeed. Without the intent to approach performance management responsibilities as an opportunity rather than a grim duty, managers create a dynamic with their direct reports that is discouraging and tension-ridden. Performance management that takes on the fear factor is ultimately and remarkably counter-productive for employees; so, rather than being a regular occasion for growth and improvement, the entire process becomes an HR exercise without a true outcome.

An anchor of the Lemon organisation concept is managers and leaders operating in their business relationships from an Adult perspective. This way of functioning as a manager and leader is part of every aspect of the role of people who manage others and people at the top of the company house. For some, what I call the Adult mode of interaction is natural and consistently present in their day-to-day interchanges; but for others, it is a struggle to pull themselves out of the habits of looking at the actions of their direct reports from a Parental point of view. It has a self-replicating tendency to plunge the recipient into the Child state ... basically, when your boss treats you like a misbehaving Child, even the most centred individual will have trouble responding with an Adult attitude. Left unchecked, it deteriorates relationships and plunges productivity to new lows.

Coaching, itself one of the key responsibilities of managers in high-performing organisations, essential to helping direct reports hone their skills, define and meet their stretch objectives, and develop a business version of the kinesthetic awareness of an athlete. The nature of coaching requires the objectivity, openness, and supportiveness of an Adult approach. A Parental Tell — Do dynamic destroys the coaching process and makes the achievement of self-awareness an impossibility ... being told what you are doing wrong and should be doing instead removes the thinking process. The manager acting as Parent demands, by his assumption of the Parental language, attitude and demeanor, compliance rather than self-discovery and the acceptance of personal responsibility for action. Where is the growth opportunity for the direct report? "Do as I say or else" has never been motivating and it still isn't.

Like coaching, giving constructive as opposed to destructive feedback requires the Adult mode. Feedback is intimidating for nearly everyone ... both the giver and the receiver. It's naturally tough to tell someone what you think of their performance, most particularly if it isn't of the quality that is expected of that person. Many managers have a lot of difficulty separating the person from the action when giving feedback, so what they say comes out as a degradation of the individual rather than objective information on the direct report's performance. Furthermore, nearly everyone has trouble hearing that their performance isn't up to par, so the dynamic is set up that creates dread coupled with defensiveness within both the giver and receiver of the feedback. Feedback that will help the receiver address the issue without feeling demoralised and attacked simply must be given by a person capable of speaking and acting as an Adult. Nothing good can come from Parent-driven feedback.

Finally, we explore the phenomenon of difficult people. There are a lot of them in business ... some more difficult than others ... but all of it is manageable if the Manager knows how to identify the difficulty and has a command of the techniques that will effectively re-channel an attitude or habit of behaviour or defuse a potentially volatile situation. From indecisiveness to bullying, managers will have to deal with it all, at one time or another. Again, the only way to approach these people who are acting like children is to be an Adult in the way you deal with them. The Parental approach will only perpetuate the problem and keep the employee in an immature cycle of behaviour. Borrow patience from your Parental tendencies, but stop there ... concentrate on coaching your direct reports to increase their awareness of their own strengths and capabilities.

Ultimately, being a Lemon manager, leader or employee draws upon and reflects the confidence, self-knowledge and self-awareness of high-performing individuals.

The Monkey Syndrome

THE MORE YOU GET RID OF YOUR PEOPLE'S MONKEYS, THE MORE TIME YOU HAVE FOR YOUR PEOPLE
... William Oncken, Jr.

The Business Monkeys

William Oncken introduced the idea of the Monkey Syndrome in his classic *Harvard Business Review* article, published in 1974. "Managing Management Time: Who's Got the Monkey?" has become a timeless lesson for leaders and managers in how not to take on the responsibilities of your employee's problems. A "Monkey" is the NEXT MOVE, a symbol of the action to be taken to move a project forward, solve the problem, or set the future direction. A manager winds up with the monkey whenever an employee brings in a problem without a solution and the manager takes on the problem, promising to take action — to **make the next move**. This may be as simple as the manager saying he will think about it, with the intention of getting back to the direct report at a later date with instructions on how to proceed. Nevertheless, the monkey jumps from the direct report's back to the manager's back the moment the manager agrees to "think about it" and stays with the manager until he is able to shift the responsibility for the next move back to the direct report.

> A "Monkey" is the NEXT MOVE ... a symbol of the action to be taken to move a project forward, solve the problem or set future direction.

The principle point is that the manager eats up his own discretionary time — that time not imposed upon him by his boss or by the system — by taking the direct report's monkey, thereby turning his discretionary time into direct report-imposed time: hardly a productive situation. The result of this shifting of monkey's leaves the manager with no time to assess performance, guide, or coach his team and no time to handle his own priorities.

Seeing that direct report A was able to pass the care and feeding of his monkey to the manager, direct report B jumps into the fray, eagerly seeking to share his issues and encourage his own monkey to jump ship for the cushy lifestyle of manager-provided food and shelter. You can see the problem here ... as direct reports get the message that their manager seems to be willingly taking over the nutritional needs of everyone's monkeys, the line of people outside the manager's door increases exponentially. The manager can easily find herself with a multitude of screaming monkeys sitting in the middle of her desk and her discretionary time dwindled down to zero. In fact, the possibility of ever being able to actually manage in a meaningful way becomes slimmer by the hour as the monkeys wreak havoc on her desk.

The monkey analogy is a very effective way of pointing out that managers who find themselves with 50 screaming monkeys on their desks have been unable to transfer the initiative back to their direct reports. The manager becomes the focal point for all future action, the focus of each direct report's quest for information and affirmation that she has taken the action she promised. When she is legitimately overwhelmed and finds herself being the roadblock to progress, she sets herself up for criticism by her direct reports who can't move forward without her instructions. In the end, her own productivity is compromised and she creates an intensely frustrating situation for herself. She also runs the risk that her own management skills could be questioned by her bosses as they see her effectiveness reduced by too much on her plate to cover it all.

Identifying Monkeys

A *Monkey* goes along with every problem, project or initiative and takes the form of decisions, direction and solutions.

Sometimes it's hard to recognise the monkey as it flies through the air from back to back, desk to desk, so let's get this straight. A monkey, being any **next action** that needs to be taken, goes along with every problem, project or initiative. It takes the form of a decision that needs to be made, a direction that needs to be given to another person or group, a solution to a pending problem ... even a phone call or a promise to think about something. A sure-fire way to anticipate the potential for monkey-shifting is a direct report who shows up unexpectedly (without an appointment, the time is convenient for him, but not for you), stops you in the corridor, catches you in the middle of a conversation with someone else while your attention is directed elsewhere, or in any other way gets close enough that his monkey is leaning out with reaching arms, looking for a new care-taker.

The minute the manager finds himself saying anything close to "I'll think about it and get back to you" he should know that the monkey is in the air soaring overhead to his back. And that monkey will stay with the manager until the initiative and responsibility for action is transferred back to the direct report.

Symptoms of Monkey Behaviour

The Monkey Syndrome in full bloom leaves managers angry at themselves for taking the monkeys and angry at direct reports for failing to take the initiative, "step up to the plate" and perform up to expectations. Direct reports, on the other hand, are clueless that there is a problem, since from their perspective; the manager has willingly taken the monkey. They feel quite justified in temporarily checking out of the action loop and later in "responsibly" checking up on the manager's progress with their monkeys. They probably are mystified at either the manager's lack of progress or his attitude about it, or both. Let's pause a minute and think about this. Who, exactly, is the boss here? Who should be checking on the progress of whom? Every time the manager takes the monkey — adopts the next move in his direct report's problem/project/role as his own — he has inadvertently switched roles, because the direct report is thus waiting for the manager to complete his task. Naturally, the direct report will not want to appear to forget about the situation or the anticipated action, so all he can do is check in with the manager periodically to see how it's going. This role reversal is a blatant symptom of the Monkey Syndrome and should be a flashing red light to the manager that the weight he feels on his shoulders is, indeed, a monkey that should not be there. (Somehow they pick up weight as they jump back and forth from back to back.)

Interestingly, the Monkey Syndrome goes hand in hand with a Tell and Do, command and control style of management. This style was particularly troublesome in the mid-1970's, because managers were being asked to do more and more with less and less, and had been employing the traditional military-inspired command and control leadership process for many years. While managers and leaders have learned much over the years about more effective management methods and largely have embraced the value of inspiring their direct reports to greater levels of empowerment, responsibility, and performance, the Monkey Syndrome is nevertheless still a problem because managers continue to allow themselves to take over the care and feeding of their direct reports' monkeys. Put another way, managing time is not any easier now than it has ever been, and now there are even more ways to drain a manager's pool of discretionary time.

Let's simplify. Here are symptoms of the Monkey Syndrome behaviour among managers.

- The manager allows herself to be drawn into discussions at a time and place where an appropriate decision can't be made, necessitating only the temporary disposition of the monkey, and delaying the real action.

Unfortunately, the temporary disposition of the monkey amounts to the monkey jumping onto the manager's back, chattering to be fed.

- The manager is drawn into a situation, again at an inopportune time or place, which was clearly the responsibility of the direct report and does not have enough information to make a quick decision. More time and more information is required by the manager before the monkey can be fed and watered, but the direct report has cast doubts in the mind of the manager about his ability to care for the monkey so the manager feels forced to assume monkey-sitting responsibility until sufficient information is available to redirect the monkey back to the direct report. This can turn into hours or days of back and forth between the manager and the direct report, during which time the manager continues to feed and water the monkey.

- The manager feels compelled to work harder and longer in order to send the monkeys back to their rightful caretakers, further reducing his effectiveness at handling his personal responsibilities and drastically limiting his ability to have the energy or time for coaching and teaching. Managers even find themselves working overtime, cutting into their personal and family time, in order to try to catch up on their boss and system-generated priorities and attempt to keep all the monkeys fed and tended. What actually happens is that the manager ends up shuffling monkeys around on his desk, with few concrete results. They all chatter and scream for attention, and their rightful owners keep vigil — just inside of the manager's field of vision to ensure the manager doesn't forget about them. The manager, on the other hand, gets further behind and more irritated by the hour.

The economic challenges of the 21st century put pressure on managers to deliver.

Probably the best clue to the circumstances that lead to the Monkey Syndrome is found in today's business environment, where productivity is king, stretch objectives are routine, and managers are **still** doing more and more with less and less. The economic challenges of the 21st century put more pressure on managers to deliver, most of whom developed professionally during the peak of the command and control management style. As corporate pressure on managers increases, the tendency to rely on what you know best and are most comfortable with becomes greater. At the same time, it is easy to slip out of the adult manager role and into a manager as Parent role during times of stress, and with the ever-present economic and political realities of recent years, managers have been stressed a **lot** of the time. The manager as Parent role is one that, for many, has been practised regularly as their children grew up. They found it worked well for them — naturally — because it is the rightful role of the parent raising children. It also happens to be a perfect model for monkey behaviour. Parents have the final word. They typically make all the decisions, or at least reserve the right to reverse any ill-conceived decision the child has made in order to protect him, and the rest of the family, from embarrassment or harm. The parent, after all, carries the monkey most of the time until the child grows up and leaves home ... some continue to carry it even after the child is an adult and has long since left to gather his own bananas. In fact, many parents find this role so natural and comfortable that they have a hard time adjusting to their grown child's desire to carry her own monkeys. Adopting the parent role, then, can be a comforting approach for parents who find their own parent role no longer appropriate with their children. This doubtless happens very subconsciously — no one would make a deliberate decision to begin taking over an employee's business decisions in an effort to recreate a role they can no long play at home.

Whatever the conscious or subconscious motivation a manager has for usurping a direct report's rightful decision-making and initiative-taking, it results in nothing but overwork for the manager and disempowerment for the direct report.

Ineffective Monkey Behaviours of Managers and Leaders

I find it is not unusual for managers to withhold decision-making from their direct reports, and setting themselves up to become the keeper of all monkeys for everyone. This limits the managers' effectiveness at coaching and developing their teams because it consumes their time and redirects their energies. At the same time, direct reports are losers as well, because their opportunity to grow, achieve and advance professionally is severely hampered by managers who withhold decision-making and action-taking.

Although to this point, the focus up to now largely has been on describing managers and the Monkey Syndrome, leaders have an even more crucial need to avoid monkey behaviour. The titular leader of an organisation — the Managing Director, CEO, Chairman — is also susceptible to the challenge of leaping monkeys. In fact, the possibility of hundreds landing on a senior manager's desk is overwhelming. Leaders at any level within the organisation, whether they manage people or not, are all potential monkey handlers. At any point, a direct report, also at any level, can present a problem, decision-making dilemma or crisis of enormous proportions. Monkey behaviour exhibited by leaders probably is more insidious and damaging to an organisation than in managers because without the creation and promulgation of a clear mission and vision for the future of the enterprise, it is possible for an entire organisation to get lost in the execution and forget the bottom line.

It isn't a failure to develop and reinforce a mission statement that creates the problem. The problem lies in leaders who allow themselves to get so embroiled in the day-to-day decision-making that they neglect their roles as visionaries and forget to articulate the higher purposes of the organisation and keep them top-of-mind for everyone ... employees need to understand the overall direction of the company, especially in today's fast-paced and complex global economy. Understanding how their individual roles contribute to the success of the whole, and having a clear line of sight between their actions and the bottom line, is critical to maintaining productivity, employee satisfaction and shareholder value.

Studies have shown that empowered and motivated employees are more productive and successful employees...

... naturally, successful employees make for a successful company. In a concrete way, workers of today are telling us that they want to believe in their leaders, but to be able to do that they need to understand why decisions are made and how those decisions impact the expectations management has for individuals. They also are willing to demand meaningful explanations and clear-cut direction, along with periodic clarification of how the company is doing and whether financial objectives are being met. And they want roles that are challenging and allow individuals to take the initiative and be responsible for the outcomes. Command and control techniques at the top levels of management stifle entrepreneurship, appropriate risk-taking and creativity all the way down the line.

Command and control techniques used by those at top levels of management stifle entrepreneurship, appropriate risk-taking and creativity.

What many of us don't realise is that we not only pick up the Parental style from our childhood experiences, we also copy the style from our business experiences. We mistakenly believe that the Tell – Do style we observe in other managers is correct and appropriate, and we adopt the style as our own when we become managers. Fundamentally the multiplication effect of Parental managers infested with Monkey Syndrome equates to a culture of command and control — in other words the issue of the Monkey Syndrome and/or Parental Management is cultural and it grows rapidly with cell-dividing speed in some organisations. It will take a conscious effort to choose to abandon both and adopt the more effective, more empowering and more fulfilling Adult style. It will also take time and a sincere personal dedication to becoming a better manager and leader.

Why Managers and Leaders Succumb to the Monkey Syndrome

Managers whom I have coached often have a number of reasons for holding decision-making close to the chest, thereby nurturing their tendencies to become everyone's monkey care giver. Taken at face value, all have something of a ring of truth.

1. They say they just don't trust their direct reports. For one reason or another, they feel that person is unable to make a wise business decision so the decision must be made for him. Naturally, the monkey lives on the manager's back where daily feeding is possible ... can't have the monkey getting sick from the wrong food.

2. Managers tell me they feel that their personal responsibility for the success of the department/project/initiative is so great that the future of their own career is riding on every action that is taken. Few are willing to leave this in the hands of any direct report when they see the outcome as such a career-breaker or -maker.

3. Other managers say that they recognise that empowering employees to succeed is their sincere management objective, but actually getting out of the way so their people can do their jobs, is exceedingly difficult. Many feel grounded in the details of their business and find it difficult to switch gears to the more strategic type of thinking and acting that comes with management responsibility. Having an opportunity to care for that monkey gives them a chance to get back to the nuts and bolts of the business they long to control.

4. Some find that their concerns about a direct report's real desire to take responsibility, to take on the care and feeding of their own monkey, are quite legitimate. Truly, not everyone who isn't in a management position wants to accept full responsibility for any given outcome. This presents the manager with a dilemma – he must discover what it will take to influence and motivate that person to stretch out of their comfort zone. Sometimes, they tell me, it's just quicker and easier not to, because their plates are so full they don't have the time to coach and teach.

I said earlier that, at face value, these reasons have a ring of truth. The downside is that the behaviours which follow from these situations are self-limiting, with negative consequences for both managers and direct reports. The familiarity of shouldering the monkey for the manager and the discomfort of the monkey for the direct report keep both stuck in a pattern that allows neither to achieve their objectives. Being saddled with screaming monkeys, however voluntarily the manager went into it, keeps the manager stuck in parent-mode, as the ultimate maker of every decision, solver of every problem and resolver of every conflict.

Lessons Learned

Not long ago I ran a training programme for a group of Senior Managers. One manager in particular had been in post for about six months. During that time she received criticism for her management style in the form of negative 360 degree feedback. The problem that was uncovered in her 360 feedback was a lack of direction. She was bewildered by this feedback because, in her view, she was giving her direct reports rather constant attention.

In reality, she had fallen into two fundamental Monkey Syndrome behaviours that she erroneously saw as positive.

- First, she allowed monkeys to literally camp out on her desk! She was seduced by a classic problem that I call "desk hangers" — direct reports primarily, although there were peers as well, that constantly hung around her desk looking for advice, approval and her opinion. Thinking she was providing direction and support to her team, she allowed these people to steal hours and hours of her working time every week. What she actually was doing was displaying the Parental behaviour of taking on the Monkeys ... lots of them. As this repeating pattern became a habit it promoted their display of Learned Helplessness.

  The more severe cases of Learned Helplessness were exemplified by the "can I just have 5 minutes brigade." These were the people who would stop by her desk asking for 5 minutes, which invariably became an hour of her time. Often during these sessions she was extracted from her desk into a meeting room or coffee area to discuss the "5 minute" issues, from which, many minutes later, she would be unable to extricate herself. Most of these incidents were legitimately task or project related. However, these situations had a way of devolving into emotional advice sessions on topics ranging from complaints about other team members to personal problems.

- The second Monkey Syndrome behaviour she unconsciously displayed was perhaps the cause of behaviour number one. Every Monday she held what she termed a "coaching session" with each team member. After asking her to walk me through how these sessions worked, we found that they were, in truth, prescriptive and not coaching sessions at all. Her approach was of the "this is what I want you to do and how I want you to do it" nature, leaving her team members with lists and lists of actions they needed to take before the following Monday. Rather than coaching her team to take the initiative and identify responsible steps for handling their projects or tasks, she dictated every step they would take.

Here are the primary problems that demonstrate clearly the Parent mode in which she was managing her team:

- Often the sessions went on for an exhausting 90 to 120 minutes each.

- This Manager spent most of the time "inspecting" the quality of the previous weeks effort by the team member and then discussing how she would have dealt with things better than they did or how they should improve their performance the next week.

- The Manager viewed her methods as good coaching, giving good direction.

In addition to all this "coaching" time she was bestowing on her team members, she was working easily 9 to 10 hours a day, every day. "How could that effort not be recognised? How can they say I don't give them clear direction when I spend so much time with them?" she bleated.

This Manager had a very forceful nature. She was an assertive woman, who actually came across as semi-aggressive, managing a mostly female team who were rather unassertive. Her various strategies only encouraged Monkey Syndrome and her manner had a very controlling effect on her team — so much so that they were trapped in their unassertive pattern and were not being coached to get out of it. Unfortunately for her, this Manager was developing a reputation for her aggressive, Tell – Do approach, which had not only her team, but also her peers and her line manager questioning her competence.

While she thought she was "coaching" she was doing exactly the opposite, and she was totally confused. After all, she was just emulating the behaviour of her own manager who was a classic Tell and Do Parent type. She was replaying the style she observed in her manager and became entrenched in the Monkey Syndrome because of it.

The limiting factor for organisations seeking to sustain a workforce that is empowered, energised and focused is that the actions of managers who fall into this kind of ineffective monkey behaviour are continually in conflict with their objectives as managers. It is virtually impossible to inspire employees to greater achievement by stretching, taking risks and maturing professionally at the same time you are approving every action before they take it and barring them from assuming their rightful responsibilities.

What Happens to Employees

When a direct report's rightful decision-making and initiative is subsumed repeatedly by a manager — when damaging monkey behaviour becomes the norm — the result can change the course of her career. It creates doubt in her mind about her own abilities to perform ... after all, the manager is clearly sending the message that the direct report isn't trusted, isn't capable and is there only to take orders. Rather than concentrating on playing to her strengths and coaching her to improve areas of potential, the manager who is willing to solve all problems and be responsible for outcomes has no time to manage performance so the direct report falls into the role of waiting for orders and directions, unable to take the initiative or handle the known and unknown events that occur in her everyday business world.

The role, and career, of a direct report working for a manager with the Monkey Syndrome devolves into one with little self-determination and growth potential because he must repeatedly stifle his own initiative. In that role, he:

- Conforms to the demands of the manager

- Becomes stuck in neutral waiting for the manager to give direction before taking any action

- Is prohibited from independent action for fear of operating at cross purposes to the manager

- Loses self-respect when his rightful areas of responsibility are encroached upon

- Has little motivation to push his boundaries or achieve independent success outside the sphere of the manager; in fact, he may be discouraged, implicitly or explicitly, from doing so by the manager

- Eventually develops an attitude problem — either one of apathy for the work or one of antipathy for the manager since there is nothing he can do to increase his level of self-determination and take responsibility for doing his job.

The direct report who promotes the Monkey Syndrome in his manager by repeatedly seeking to abandon her monkeys to the manager's care — and who has a manager that falls into the Monkey Syndrome — eventually suffers from what we call learned helplessness. When he gets positive reinforcement from the manager for monkey shifting, as exemplified by the evidence of the manager's desk full of monkeys, he almost becomes unable to carry his own monkey and manage its diet. In other words, he learns that his manager will accept, or possibly demand, that the initiative rest with the manager, and without the ability to make decisions, solve problems and even fulfill the responsibilities of his position he gradually becomes the helpless, hapless order-taker, forever waiting on the manager to give the next direction.

Lessons Learned

I worked with a PhD, named "Steve" for purposes of this book, who was one of the few, if not the only person in the whole Country, with the technical competence to deliver the technical requirements of the project on which he was working. He was a brilliant and intelligent individual. However, he had a problem: his own manager, his HR department and many previous managers had tried to get him to see the light — but he was stubborn.

Here was the problem: he had this inability to manage people — he was totally a Parental Tell and Do type of manager. Actually, he was only given the departmental manager role as a way of recognising his importance to the whole organisation. Equally problematic ... he was a complete Prima Donna. The team only really survived because of one strong character who displayed Lemon behaviours. The team looked to this person as a surrogate leader, without whom it would have disintegrated long before.

In addition to his Tell and Do ways, he just expected people to know what to do — to know what direction they were supposed to be going in — to know how to develop themselves. Basically, management was an evil to him — a second class citizen. The centre of his world was in being the best, the only person who could do "it," and he was continually frustrated by what he considered as the inadequacies of others. The net effect was that the team suffered, it was directionless, and it had experienced a downward spiral of morale. This team was missing out on new projects because they were perceived to be able to barely handle the work they had and to not have the capacity to take on anything new. As time progressed, this situation worsened.

Initially, I was called in to coach him out of his attitude and Parental management style, but this proved as fruitless for me as other people's previous efforts. Although we achieved small improvements, he simply wouldn't or couldn't change.

It was understanding whether it was *wouldn't* or *couldn't* that provided the central solution. A "won't" do situation is a lack of willingness or motivation to change. I knew that if it ended up that he *wouldn't* do anything about it, we had some serious considerations to make regarding his future as a Manager. However, removing him from the managerial role would have been momentous as he would have definitely sulked like a Child (he, by the way, had a preference to do the Parent/Child switch when he didn't get his own way). Further, because of his technical competence, there were concerns that, if confronted, he may well have left the company. This would have created a huge issue for the company, including the loss of major projects, and as a consequence, company revenue in the future.

The "can't do" situation is caused by a lack of training, knowledge or ability and can usually be fixed through the right solution – though the art is knowing which one! I decided to challenge the "can't do" symptoms by asking him to change from doing work in "his way" to doing work in "my way." He agreed. We discussed and agreed on what the behaviours and consequences were of his way. Then I asked him to do it my way for a two week period. I was with him for the first two days, and then spoke to him on the phone for twenty minutes every other day during this time.

Bottom-line — I asked him to adopt an Adult style and BE a Manager. Because of his stubbornness, the majority of the initial two days were spent with me in high instruction / Adult mode myself. I had to do this to get through his thick skin and get him to listen. After that, I was able to encourage him to follow me into being an Adult and display more and more Lemon attributes.

The more he practiced Adult behaviours and displayed Lemon attributes the greater the changes he underwent. He responded to my modeled behaviour and became more and more comfortable with that behaviour in himself. The net effect was that, in just 2 weeks, he came to understand how to get more done through and with his people in the Adult mode. Not surprisingly, it still took him several more weeks to change the perception others had of him and for his new found Adult style to "gel." Only by PROVING to him the rewards of his new Lemon approach did he believe their effectiveness and did he and others see that he COULD do it.

Identifying and Changing Monkey Behaviour

Many managers have no idea they are locked in an internal struggle between what they intend and what they instigate. They proceed with the parent-focused behaviour that sets up their direct reports for adaptive child responses. What may be misleading here is that word "adaptive." Adaptive responses can be represented as either compliant or defiant ... and in business neither attitude is particularly constructive. When a transaction between the manager and direct report is conducted in the Parent – Child mode, neither the manager nor the direct report is able to give their best. The manager in Parent mode is often judgmental and demanding, operating in a commanding Tell and Do fashion: the attitude of a nurturing parent is generally viewed as too "soft" for business. The direct report exhibiting the adaptive child behaviour will either acquiesce with resentment at the attitude of the manager, or fight back, figuratively or literally. In the end, the communication between the manager and direct report is marred by the poor attitudes and conflicting thoughts elicited in both of them. Unless one of them makes drastic changes in their habits of interaction, the situation and relationship between them will continue to deteriorate. Rectifying this is really the responsibility of the manager for the simple reason that she has the fate of the employee in her hands and the power to change the manner of interaction between her direct report and herself by changing her own approach. By changing her manner of interaction to the Adult perspective, she will set up the employee to be able to respond in an adult way. Look at the following scenario.

Manager Jones has previously had an open relationship with Direct report Simmons. In the past, Simmons has appeared to make fairly good decisions, and when Jones has made suggestions as to alternative action, Simmons has successfully either accepted the suggestion or countered with a logical alternative. Then Jones has a really bad day. She gets a load of bad news, has a confrontation with an unjustifiably angry board member, and is put in the position of having to defend a direct report who dropped the ball. Normally, any of these wouldn't faze Jones, but she has just returned from a long journey filled with traffic jams and road rage. Her patience is at an end — a position in which parents sometimes find themselves. If she doesn't watch it, in an effort to take control of her environment which she feels is temporarily out of control, she will set up a chain reaction of Parent – Child behaviour.

Here's how it could happen. Simmons, unaware of all that has taken place in the life of his manager, drops into Jones' office unannounced to share a problem. Simmons has a solution in the back of his mind, but thinking that he will outline the situation before presenting the solution, he launches into a lengthy description of the problem without first taking the mental temperature of his boss. After the few days Jones has had, this is the last thing she wants at that moment ... and from her perspective Jones is behaving like her 12 year old child who drops the "I need this tomorrow" bomb on her frequently and at the least opportune moments.

You can see where this probably is going, can't you? Jones is in no mood to listen to what she interprets as a diatribe from Simmons against the person and situation he is attempting to describe. She does what is tantamount to telling him to shut up and sends him to his room with the admonition that she will deal with him and his problem later. (Oops, she just took the monkey!) Jones, on the other hand, is shocked by her response to his story and isn't given a chance to present his own solution or assure her he has everything under control. He is offended and abashed, realising he could have set this whole thing up better and should have checked on how her journey went before jumping into the current problem on his plate. While he may realise he could have done things differently, he is so irritated with her reaction that he stomps out of the room, determined to punish her for her shabby treatment of him. I won't go through the whole bloody siege, but suffice it to say that they continue down the Parent – Child path, neither able to pull themselves back into the adult business world until Jones finally gets some sleep and realises that she has to put a stop to both of their reactions. This is a turning-point for Jones, who, as the manager, holds the fate of this relationship in her hands. Even if Simmons makes an effort to go back to their normal Adult – Adult transaction mode, unless Jones is willing to let go of her parental (punitive and controlling) attitude, he won't be able to change the situation. Simmons, on the other hand, can pull Jones back into the adult world because she can change the nature of their transactions by doing two things:

1. Jones must change the way she thinks about what Simmons is telling her, she must stop judging and giving orders, and she must talk with Simmons reasonably without trying to control the situation and without reacting emotionally.

2. If Jones stops to remember that Simmons is usually a very responsible individual with typically good ideas, she will be able to relax and let him get back to normal. She has to give the monkey back to him and let him feed it. As long as she keeps his monkey, he can only wait for her to make the next move. In other words, she needs to ask for his recommendation on how to handle the situation, listen calmly and acknowledge that it is his responsibility. If she has direction she wants to give, she must do so reasonably and calmly, as any rational adult would ... as she normally would.

How can they both prevent their interactions from ever spiraling out of control again? They can by staying grounded in their own personalities. In this example, both the manager and the direct report slipped out of their normal modes of operation, out of their typical behaviour patterns. (This shifting out of norm is a stress reaction, it occurs easily, with alarming swiftness, and often with disastrous consequences.) They will again find themselves at the ends of their respective ropes, but this event could be a vivid reminder of how they **don't** want to react. Jones needs to recognise when she is at a breaking point with the stress of her position, and allow herself to refuse a problem-solving session with a direct report. She can do this reasonably and calmly by simply stopping the direct report before he gets going with his story and letting him know she would like to defer the discussion until a later time. She will need to remember to specify a later time so Simmons won't misconstrue this as a brush-off. On the other hand, Simmons needs to be more astute and aware that his manager, whom he likes and respects, has a position of responsibility. He can promote her confidence in him by reading the "moment" and by focusing on his approach to the solutions rather than appearing to dump his problems on her. This can be as easy as simply telling her he has a solution he wants to present, before he starts into the background story. He even may find that she will trust his judgment enough that he can pare down the litany of details he is prepared to give her to the basics of the case, saving both of them valuable time and increasing his confidence in his own ability to handle his area of responsibility.

Abandoning monkey behaviour in favour of an Adult interaction style isn't the easiest thing to do. As with Jones and Simmons, it will mean the difference between a downwardly spiraling relationship that will eventually self-destruct and a successful one in which Jones leads by example and her actions breed successful, productive direct reports.

The Care and Feeding of Monkeys

The monkey metaphor for managing time is about maintaining a balance between ensuring the direct report is able to take the initiative for managing his own monkeys and taking over monkey management from her. It comes with a "how to" guide in regard to managing the monkey population that springs from any set of direct reports and to

> **The fact of business life is there will always be Monkeys ... effective management behaviour depends on the managers willingness to transfer the initiative.**

keeping the manager in control of her discretionary time. Far from controlling the actions and results of direct reports, managers must focus on coaching, encouraging and requiring direct reports to take responsible actions within the parameters of their positions.

To avoid being overcome by the Monkey Syndrome, there are six compulsory principles for managing the care and feeding of monkeys.

Principle 1. No monkeys can be allowed to languish on your back or your desk. You must take action else you will waste valuable time dealing with them and trying to keep them alive.

Principle 2. While direct reports will gladly pile the monkeys on your desk, or your back, you must keep them under control. You can never take on more monkeys than you can feed and dispose of in less than 15 minutes. Ideally, monkey disposition should be immediate because you are able to feed it the minute it springs into the air, thereby insuring that it will land back on the direct report's lap.

Principle 3. Never go hunting for monkeys. If your direct report is caring for the Monkey, let him; and if your direct report needs your support in his care and feeding of the monkey, he should do so by appointment only … no stopping in the corridor or dropping into your office unannounced. You will need to train your direct reports in an appropriate way to respect your time and their own.

Principle 4. Always feed monkeys in person. This keeps the monkey where it belongs, on the back of your direct report, and it cuts down the amount of time you both spend in feeding. Never try to feed a monkey by phone or email because the next move will always revert back to you. While it is good to document your agreement or approval of the monkey (Next Step), it should never be the mechanism for Monkey care.

Principle 5. Define clearly the next step to be taken for every monkey, as well as who is responsible and the degree of initiative. You always have the option to agree with your direct report on a revised next step, but if you leave it vague and undefined you can count on the same monkey landing back on your desk, screaming.

Principle 6. Use the Adult style when dealing with your direct report and her monkeys. If you slip into the Parent style, your direct report will be confused or feel brow-beaten. Your objective is for your direct report to take over monkey disposition, but if she feels she is merely doing as she has been told, there will be no personal reward in it for her to take the initiative. To permanently become adept at monkey management, she needs to feel she is successfully living up to her role and that you trust her to do her job because she has proven her good judgment and abilities.

The fact of corporate life is that there will always be monkeys: problems will always need disposition and projects will always need action to move forward. Whether a manager is prepared to exhibit effective management behaviour, thus avoiding the Monkey Syndrome, is dependent on whether he is willing to transfer the initiative to his direct reports, to give up some direct control over tasks and decisions, and to trust his direct reports' abilities to do the jobs for which they were hired.

Key Points Summary

> Monkeys are a metaphor for any action that is waiting to be taken.

> Monkeys don't care on whose back they ride — they will happily jump from direct report to manager, screaming for attention.

> Monkeys can be seen flying through the air toward any manager who allows himself to be derailed from controlling his own discretionary time.

➢ A manager gives up control of her discretionary time when she becomes the focal point for the next action upon which her direct reports must wait before they can move forward.

➢ Monkey behaviour is a partner to manager-as-Parent behaviour where the manger takes a command and control attitude and direct reports are expected to follow orders, relinquishing their role to initiate action (make decisions, solve problems).

➢ Both managers and direct reports are responsible for the creation of ineffective monkey behaviour, but the manager has the responsibility to recognise it and change the manner of transaction with the direct report from Parent – Child to Adult – Adult.

➢ The manager who does not want to be confounded by the Monkey Syndrome must learn to recognise flying monkeys, become adept at deflecting them, and build trust with their direct reports. They must force themselves to step back and refuse to be pulled into monkey management in order to have the discretionary time to focus on the performance of their teams and create an environment where direct reports are able to take the initiative, make decisions, and complete organisational transactions.

Management Lemons

THE ULTIMATE MEASURE OF GREAT LEADERS IS THAT THEY DEVELOP A SET OF FOLLOWERS WHO ARE EQUIPPED TO TAKE OVER.

... Lee Gilbert

What's a Lemon?

The concept of a business Lemon is the opposite of that of a Monkey. While a monkey signifies the loss of discretionary time and the negative behaviour associated with taking on inappropriate responsibility for direct report's initiative for action, a Lemon has zest and is symbolic of energy, enthusiasm, confidence, a willingness to learn, a readiness to act and a positive attitude. Any manager who exhibits Lemon attributes leads with ease, generates enthusiasm for both the direction and the steps her organisation is taking, recognises and trusts the strengths and capabilities of her team and gets out of the way so they can do their jobs, and controls the things that interrupt her focus and cause her to be unable to concentrate on the needs of her team. A direct report who exhibits Lemon attributes is eager to take responsibility and fulfill the potential of her position, presents well thought out solutions and is confident in solving her own problems, and knows when and how to ask for help so that her ability to make good business judgments is never in question. Put together, this is the best possible combination of attitude, approach and purpose.

Empowerment is a FEELING not an ACTION.

Lemons also have the ability to stimulate empowerment in others and to take empowerment from their own managers/leaders. Empowerment has been written about and discussed with vigor. It is a focal topic for many management experts and has been measured and tested in a wide variety of environments. It is important, however, to understand that empowerment is a FEELING not an ACTION. No manager one can empower a direct report. What she **can** do is to set up the mode of interaction within the team in such a way that individual initiative is nurtured, encouraged and expected. By her behaviour — when she exhibits a trusting, coaching and Adult attitude and approach — she is enabling her direct reports to feel empowered to act, to hang onto those monkeys and to be completely responsible for their care and feeding. It is her leadership that makes it possible by creating the atmosphere for empowerment. When we test environments for the level of employee empowerment, we will never find it where managers and leaders are operating in the Tell –Do Parent mode. No employee will feel empowered when they must wait upon the manager for direction and approval or disapproval before action can be initiated. The Monkey Syndrome is not conducive to employee empowerment. Rather, it is the breeding ground for learned helplessness and employee dissatisfaction.

Again and again, studies conducted by all sorts of consulting companies and institutes have repeatedly shown that employees are not engaged and will not expend any discretionary effort for their organisation when they feel their managers control their every move. Managers operating with a Parental Tell – Do mentality are delegating the next move, and by maintaining control for the care and feeding of monkeys they create an environment that is the exact opposite of one which stimulates the empowerment of their direct reports. While empowerment strategies include open communication and encourage dialogue and sharing of opinions and thoughts between managers and direct reports, most delegation strategies block or dismiss input from the direct report. Managers who are taught to be "good delegators" will be forever locked in the Monkey Syndrome because they will become incapable of allowing their direct reports to think for themselves, and their direct reports will become powerless and fearful of acting without the direction of their manager. Never confuse the management of monkeys and the control of the Monkey Syndrome with delegation. Delegation is not the answer to screaming

Most delegation strategies used by managers block or dismiss input from the subordinate.

monkeys on the managers desk: it is the perpetuation of the Parent – Child cycle, and employees will either get fed up and leave, looking for an environment where they can progress professionally and feel respected, or they will settle into the role of submissive children who wait for their Parent to tell them what to do and whose professional self-image is determined by the approval level of the manager.

Here's a case in point of Empowerment vs. Delegation.

> Jones, who is normally an enlightened manager, has her stress under control and is back to operating in the Adult mode. She has a new project that she has just been handed by her boss. It will involve her whole team and her boss expects it to include some new techniques in customer service. To ensure her people are able to give their best efforts, she knows she must involve them from the outset. In order to draw from them their most creative and forward-thinking ideas, they must feel ownership of the end result. They must feel empowered to fully participate in the conceptualisation, planning and execution of the project. Jones realises that some risks will need to be taken in order to create and implement new techniques. She will need her people to think outside the box, and to do so they must believe she will support them and that she wants them to explore their out-of-the-box ideas. Risk-taking, therefore, is encouraged as Jones tells her team about the project and clearly defines their roles and hers. They leave their introductory meeting being clear about her expectations, their areas of responsibility and her confidence that they will exceed her boss's expectations. They feel EMPOWERED. They are inspired to expand their thinking, to push the current boundaries of customer service practices, and to create new and innovative solutions. My money is on Jones and her team to define a dynamic new vision for this company's approach to customer service.

> Consider now another manager, Powell, in a different organisation. He and his team also have been given the responsibility for creating new customer service techniques. Unlike Jones, he is not an open and confident manager, and his direct reports mistrust him and dislike his

methods. More often than not, they leave a meeting with him feeling like they have been "dumped on," as though Powell has just lined them up to shoot orders at them. After this project initiation meeting, they have no idea what the thinking is behind the project, nor do they feel Powell is being completely honest with them, either in his description of the issues facing the company or in what he ultimately expects the team to accomplish. They have been given the shortest of briefs and a list of tasks they must complete in an impossibly short time frame. Unlike Jones' team, they are not excited about the prospect of succeeding in an important endeavor for the organisation and they feel no ownership whatever of it or its outcome. Empowerment is the last thing on their minds. They know Powell is a proficient delegator and they are accustomed to being told what to do at every turn, to the point where three of them are actively looking for other jobs. The project actually scares them witless because it is high-profile and Powell has let them know that their necks are on the chopping block if it fails and that he has no intention of "taking the fall" for their incompetence. The people who leave Powell's meeting are discouraged, fearful and demoralised. He has delegated effectively, but because of his methods he actually has set them up to fail.

In which organisation would you want to work?

What Jones does successfully as a manager/leader is one of the keys to making Lemons: she creates an atmosphere of empowerment for her team. She has empowerment strategies that work:

- Jones respects and trusts her people.

- She is trustworthy — she promises to support them and upholds her promise. No one is thrown under the bus for a mistake.

- She defines her expectations and the team's roles so there are no surprises for anyone.

◆ She does not change her expectations in the middle of the project, unless she renegotiates and involves her team so it is a mutual decision.

◆ Jones clearly outlines the issues facing the company that are driving the project and creates a clear line of sight between organisational objectives and their actions.

◆ She is excited about the project and is able to get her people excited too by involving them every step of the way ... she invests them in the outcome by that involvement.

◆ She is a self-confident leader/manager and inspires their confidence in her and in themselves.

◆ Because she sets up the project so the entire team feels ownership for it, everyone is committed to making a clear and significant contribution to the project's success. When the project succeeds, they all succeed.

◆ Jones' team knows that she is not setting them up to take her orders so she can take the glory for a successful project or they can take the blame if it fails.

◆ The team knows that she is in it with them. She will be there to guide, coach, and advise them as they each handle their areas of responsibility.

In every team there is the potential to be Lemons rather than Monkeys ... it rests on the manager to set the direction with an empowerment strategy...

◆ Her enthusiasm is infectious. She is convinced of and committed to a successful project at such a level that they can only feel the same way.

The fact is, Jones is a Lemon herself. In addition to embodying the qualities of a Lemon, she is an excellent Lemon role model. Just like too many monkeys breed more monkeys – you can cultivate more and more Lemons through contagious practices. Jones encourages her direct reports to model her behaviour through her coaching techniques as well as her example. Jones is a successful manager. She is recognised repeatedly by her superiors for her team's success and she never fails to share the praise. She is rewarded for her successes, and she rewards her direct reports. She consistently celebrates the individual and collective achievements of her direct reports, and encourages their pride in themselves and their accomplishments. Jones team sees her successful attitudes and behaviours and is inspired to emulate them. This has made Jones and her team a very high profile commodity in the organisation. They thrive on challenges and have the confidence in her, themselves and each other to achieve at the highest levels.

Unfortunately, teams like Jones' are unusual. In every team there is the potential to be Lemons rather than monkeys. It rests on the manager to set the direction, to have an empowerment strategy that is well-developed and complete, and to use the strategy consistently. It needs to become the manager's way of life. No team will maintain a feeling of empowerment if the atmosphere of empowerment is fleeting and inconsistent — if it is subject to disappear or revert to Tell – Do as the stress-level of the manager increases. Successful teams operate in the world of the Lemon. You never see a Monkey as successful, while Lemons are obviously successful, and they are visible to others as successful and well regarded. Don't organisations want Lemons? Of course they do. Organisations reward and desire Lemons for all the reasons described above, but the fact is most organisations have more monkeys than Lemons. That's the problem.

So — what do you think? Do you think you have more monkeys than Lemons in your organisation? More monkeys equal an organisation with these attributes:

- Consistently falls short on business objectives and financial objectives

- Managers continuously feel over-worked and stressed out

- Employees are insecure about their positions, fear and resist change, and can be heard speaking resentfully of their managers

- Low productivity, and even lower morale

- Managers fail to deliver acceptable business results

- High staff turn-over

- Managers consistently are late with performance appraisals, or don't bother to conduct them at all

- A population that complains frequently about workload and staffing (be careful of this one — staffing may indeed be inadequate)

- Few high-performing departments or teams.

More Lemons means you have an organisation with:

- Teams who consistently exceed their financial and business objectives

- Employees who take change in stride and are eager for new challenges

- Employees who express a high level of satisfaction with their work environment, the professional development opportunities they are afforded within their teams, and the reward system

- Teams of employees who are confident in their skills and abilities and view new projects and procedures as opportunities for growth

- Managers who lead by example as measured by both their personal success and that of their direct reports

- Teams who express respect for and appreciation of their managers and leaders

- Employees who can articulate the organisation's mission and vision and are clear about its business direction

- Managers who foster a culture of learning, empowerment and high-performance.

- If you have more monkeys than Lemons ... read on.

Lessons Learned

Even in organisations that have more Lemons than Monkeys, there are still Monkey Syndrome issues – they just manifest themselves in different ways or only in certain departments. In my consultancy, I'm often asked to work with companies where I find these local cultural anomalies – companies that have a fragmented culture compared to those with a solid 'core' of living values in action. Some companies, as well, are excellent at portraying a "public persona" that creates a false impression that it's a great and empowering place to work – yet in reality, at the 'coal face,' it isn't that at all. This is especially true of larger monolithic entities that often perform well in annual employer of the year or best place to work competitions. These businesses usually suffer from Monkey Syndrome as much or more than others, but instead of choosing to deal with it they choose to mask it with pretense in a public relations exercise.

Some companies, however, have been able to face their Monkey Syndromes and successfully get past them. One client in particular comes to mind. That client has an excellent management matrix and has been able to engender a culture that supports and cultivates Lemons. Over the last few years I have helped this company to develop their Lemon culture to the point it is today by using a variety of training workshops, individual coaching and consulting.

This business achieves its results through a well formed set of corporate core values that encourage people to take both responsibility and calculated risks to deliver on stretch objectives. The cultural underpinnings are a common language based on words and phrases by which people feel empowered and a performance management system that evaluates performance not just against a competency framework, but also on how they deliver the corporate values.

This company rewards people that "raise their profile" and highlights the performance of their "stars" as role models for others to follow. This cultural position was hard fought during a period where they concentrated on culling the Monkeys. In fact, only a few years ago they had an old-style top heavy management structure – they had twice as many people as they do today but their production levels were 3 times lower than they are now. In other words with 50% of the original staff they now are producing 300% more than they were. They have achieved this by first culling those unable to get out of the Monkey Syndrome and then by managing through the change period with open and honest communication. Here are the concrete steps they took to create a new Lemon culture:

- They encouraged Managers to be honest with employees about their performance.

- They concentrated on creating a Coaching culture, working with me to model and train Coaching behaviours for many who found it unfamiliar and foreign.

- They revamped the appraisal system from one that had become merely a "box ticking" exercise into one that was actively grounded in continuous communication between manager and direct report and that became an enabler of performance excellence.

- The managers dealt with poor performance not by ignoring it or carrying the Monkeys, but instead by acknowledging performance issues, informing people of their options and encouraging poor performers to step up and take action to improve.

- They invested time in encouraging people to challenge the thinking of their bosses and the senior teams – an approach largely unheard of in such a widespread manner. This was driven by the Leaders at all levels of the business. These leaders were not just those in a senior management position, they were the "go to" people at all levels who were able to embrace this concept. The emphasis on contributory thinking moved this company away from the Parent – Child style to a true Adult – Adult style.

Casualties of a complete culture shift such as this company experienced were to be expected, and indeed they happened. Not everyone wanted to be part of a new corporate culture, and many simply did not want to change their ways. After the initial "cull" those disaffected souls left voluntarily, either because their under-performing style was exposed or because they didn't like living under and enforcing the new culture. Once completed, the business was able to get on the front foot and sorted its recruitment procedures to ensure it was bringing in people that already shared and valued the company's new core values.

With the HR and Personnel systems addressed, the culture is now sustaining itself through a perpetuation effect. As staff are being promoted into management positions they are now copying a successful Adult style rather than copying their previous managers' Parent styles. The perpetuation effect has meant that very few monkeys now occupy the air space above the desks of the management – and the once low morale and low confidence level in the business have evaporated. People at all levels are far more engaged because they understand that to be successful they have stretch objectives to deliver. They know they can reach those objectives because they feel empowered to do what it takes to reach them.

In fact when you speak to the people that were there before this transformation they express wonder as to what the other 50% were doing in the old organisation — probably directing Monkey traffic!

Modes of Interaction

Continuing with a Transactional Analysis approach to defining modes of interaction, we see both managers and direct reports interacting with each other in Parent, Adult or Child modes. Generally the manager's choice is Parent or Adult, and the direct

An Adult communicates with an attentive, interested and non-threatening demeanor.

report's choice is Child or Adult. As you saw in the first chapter, one usually will attract its opposite. When people interact from an Adult perspective they are displaying attitudes they have found to be effective in business interactions. They behave objectively and their reactions are open and natural, because an adult has learned by observation and personal experience. An adult is able to think and decide how to act based on what he has learned as an adult about how successful people behave in business. He knows Adults communicate with an attentive, interested and non-threatening demeanour, listening to the other person and responding accordingly in a reasonable manner.

When the Parent mode is evoked, a manager or leader is exhibiting behaviours that often stem from a more ingrained perspective based on childhood experience. We are instructed by the methods used by the adults around whom we grew up, and that internalised adult behaviour is taken with us into our own adulthood. Generally we either copy the behaviour or avoid it, depending on our individual responses to the way we were treated. Contingent upon the quality and content of our childhood encounters, our own parental behaviour will be influenced in either a positive or negative sense. How we behave isn't driven by whether that parental behaviour manifests itself toward children or other adults. The "voice of authority" we exhibit when operating in Parent mode is, in reality, a playback of the conditioning we received on what Parent behaviour looks like.

Individuals driven by the Child mode of interaction are reacting based on emotion. As children do, these people are not thinking about what they are saying or doing, they are merely reacting to what is put in front of them. When business people appear to be highly emotional and somewhat irrational, they are definitely dealing from a Child state. Anyone can choose to, but these people **don't** take control of their own emotional baggage. They don't stop at any time during an interaction with either a peer or superior to consider what they are doing and saying, or the potential impact their response will have on the situation and the other person. Adults in Child mode exhibit many symptoms of childish unhappiness with their plight, both verbally and in their body language. They resort to bedraggled and desperate posture and seem to lose their adult vocabulary by relying on superlatives and other words designed to impress the person with whom they are interacting with the magnitude of their point of view. You can easily spot the Child mode because it will remind you of the children in your life — especially any teenagers you see behaving like 8-year-olds. They may have the body of an adult, but the body language is definitely that of a child. As you can easily see, this is highly ineffective behaviour for an adult who expects to operate successfully in a business environment. Also, it pairs much too well with the manager-as-Parent interaction style: Parent to Child interaction pairings form a very destructive cycle that requires serious self-discipline to break.

What we've been talking about in this section is communication. Communication forms the basis for any business transaction. It is, by definition, the process of exchanging information, signals or messages by talk, gestures or writing, the end result of which is a shared understanding, language and definition. In business it is desired that communication also result in a determination of whether there are next steps, what they encompass and who should take them. The transaction created by communication is the basis of monkey behaviour and the means by which people of "Lemon" persuasion infuse into their organisation their zestful approach to business. Communication is easier between people operating in the same mode, as illustrated by the graphic below.

When two people who are interacting behave as adults, for example, their communication is parallel and they are thinking in a similar way. They will be able to perceive the attitude and 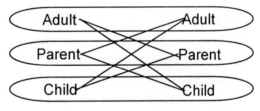 approach of the other person, creating a more comfortable transaction. This is easy to understand in the Adult — Adult pairing. However, in a business situation, while communication will be easier and more understandable between people who are both in either Parent or Child mode, it often proves to be rather unproductive. In Parent mode, both will be inclined to give orders and neither will be especially eager to take the order. Likely they will find someone else on whom to bestow the fruits of their transaction ... they will need to find a Child. Likewise, when both are playing in the Child sandbox, it will be very difficult for them to reach any kind of efficacious conclusion. They will surely seek a Parent to whom they can pass the monkey and who will make a final decision for them. While comfortable and easily understood, unless these complimentary transactions are carried out by two people in Adult position, they will fall resoundingly into the Monkey Syndrome. These are not the transactions destined to grown Lemons.

Looking at the graphic, you can easily identify the Parent – Child pairing of behaviour and you know that it will not be even partially workable if the Child behaves as acquiescent and adaptive. When transactions conducted from the perspective of Parent – Child are situational, as exemplified by the story about Jones and Simmons, the behaviour is a choice. Although it was unconscious, each made a choice, and each has the opportunity to select a new mode of behaviour at their next interaction. With these two individuals, there is a likelihood that they can successfully move back into their Adult positions.

When the manager or leader chooses to play the Parent because it is useful or comfortable, he does so to the detriment of both the direct report and the organisation. Whether by conscious choice or the unconscious playback of ingrained conditioning, the manager-as-Parent is pushing the direct report into an ineffectual position. The Parent manager is creating an environment where the likelihood is that zestful and creative capabilities never will be encouraged in his direct reports, and where he will devote his time to managing monkeys everywhere rather than to managing performance and creating a culture of personal growth and achievement. No Lemons can be possible in this organisation.

When the direct report chooses to play the Child to the manager's Parent because it is a comfortable position, he is adapting to his surroundings in the same way he did as a child. When he is thrust into the Child role because of the behaviour of his superior and this is not a comforting position for him, he can choose to change his reaction to the Adult perspective. Because the roles of Parent to Child are not parallel, this will inhibit communication and possibly thwart the transaction. Likely it will irritate the manager who is expecting compliance, and it may frustrate the direct report because adults don't appreciate being treated like children. I have coached managers who were frustrated by a direct report who fails to fall in line with his programme ... that is who won't play the compliant child and do as she is told to do. When I determine that the direct report actually is attempting to handle the situation in an Adult fashion, I know I will have to focus on helping the manager realise that his behaviour is the problem. In order to create balance within his relationship with the direct report, he will have to abandon his Parent approach and seek an Adult – Adult balance. Before he can hope to focus on managing performance and building a department of high-achieving Lemons, she will have to change his approach completely, both his habit of monkey care and his controlling Tell and Do style.

What this journey through the realm of Transactional Analysis boils down to is that, in the real world of 21st Century business relationships, managers who seek to control all the actions and decisions within their organisations will wind up with a group of ineffectual and disaffected direct reports who are incapable of doing their jobs with enthusiasm and confidence. It affects both sides of the business relationship in ways the participants can seldom recognise without help. Managers and leaders simply don't see that they can't possibly build their staffs into a group of people who are highly effective, self-directed contributors, responsibly fulfilling their roles with enthusiasm and insight at the same time they are withholding from their direct reports the decisions that are rightfully theirs and treating them as order-takers. Likewise, those who are stuck in the Parent role can't fulfill their individual potentials as inspiring and motivating leaders. They will be perpetually on the short end of discretionary time, forever managing tasks rather than people, and unable to devote any energy to coaching and giving feedback. Adults coach ... Parents instruct and prescribe. For many managers, it is much easier to instruct and prescribe than to coach because coaching requires a focus on people rather than tasks.

Managers who seek to control all the actions and decisions within their organisations will wind up with a group of ineffectual and disaffected subordinates.

Effective Management/Leadership Styles

Having identified what doesn't work particularly well within the style of transactional behaviours, let's concentrate on the Adult style, which makes both managers/leaders and their direct reports effective. Simply put, operating in the Adult style of management positions the manager to be able to fully engage in the leadership of their team/organisation, and to focus on managing people rather than managing the tasks for which their people are responsible. It keeps business transactions in the rational, thinking realm and out of the emotion-laden reaction-filled sphere of childhood experiences.

The theory behind Transactional Analysis includes the identification of physical and verbal traits inherent in each of the ego states exemplified by the three behaviour styles (Adult, Parent and Child). There are several specific physical clues that signify those who operate from an Adult perspective. These Adult traits include the following:

- Focusing attention on the other person

- Letting that person know you are interested in what they are saying through body language and facial expressions

- Maintaining a non-threatening, relaxed posture

- Adopting a non-threatened posture and expression

- In most humans, a tilted-head indicates the person is listening and processing the information being received.

In addition to physical traits, you can identify the Adult by certain verbal clues. Adults use emotion-free, objective terms when they deal with each other and direct reports, and avoid absolutes and critical, dictatorial terminology. Their language is full of comparative expressions and reasoned statements.

The verbal clues of Adult behaviour include these words and phrases:

Why	What
How	Who
Where and when	How much
In what way	In my opinion
False	True
Possibly	Probably
I realize	I see
I believe	I think

I list these because giving up the Tell and Do habits of the Parent mode in favour of operating from an Adult perspective can be learned. Managing as an Adult rather than a Parent takes concentration and hard work, but I advise my clients to start by working on the physical and verbal clues. It is the first thing that employees will recognise as you take command of a new approach to management. They will see you in a different light, "see" you listen attentively to them; and when they hear you use a more objective and open style of speaking they will have evidence that you are making a change in how you deal with them.

Let's look at the interaction between Simmons and Jones again. Here's how it could have evolved had Jones been able to get past her fatigue and learned responses to stress and demands on her time.

> Jones has the same rotten day she did in the previous story and has just returned from the same exhausting journey. However, when Simmons flops into her side chair she consciously chooses to set aside her frustration and fatigue to interact with a trusted direct report. However, she isn't in the mood for a long diatribe. She still wants to cut the story to the bottom line, but rather than lean back in her chair dismissively, she continues to exhibit Adult body language by sitting up attentively and showing her

interest by her facial expression. Being aware of her own time pressures and her need to keep her stress level from increasing, she speaks calmly and in a friendly tone. It could go something like this: "While I realise your stories are always entertaining and informative, I've had an exhausting day and just returned from that journey. I want to hear the whole thing, but until I can get some sleep, could you skip the details and give me the highlights along with what you believe is the best way to respond to this situation?" Using these words, Jones is acknowledging their history and positive relationship, and she has accepted responsibility for how she is feeling. She clearly and calmly asks for what she needs in a way that respects Jones' need to be thorough but still sets the parameters for the discussion in a way that is non-threatening and non-judgmental. She has positioned Jones, as well, to give her his recommendation at the outset. She will stop that monkey in mid air from jumping onto her desk because all she has to do is agree or redirect Simmons recommended solution, if necessary. She does not have to take on the care and feeding of his monkey or "get back to him" with any decisions. She has the shortened discussion she needs to keep her own equilibrium, and Simmons is able to summarise his situation and present his solution for her approval. Both have operated in their Adult state, and are able to meet their individual ego needs.

Sometimes the best way to reverse the habit of engaging in Parent – Child interaction is to take a hard look at your habits and behaviours. I often start out working with my clients by analysing what they consider the worst interactions, or "transactions," they can remember having with their direct reports. It's hard to face yourself when you see destructive behaviour running rampant throughout your relationships, but the result is empowering and liberating ... for both the manager and her direct reports.

Managers Should Be Leaders First

Managing is about exercising authority. Leading is about inspiring and motivating. As we've already discovered, there are nuances to the way in which authority is assigned and practiced: it can be enthusiastic and inspiring or embroiled in task tending. Further, while all leaders aren't managers of groups of people, shouldn't all managers aspire to be leaders? It is my belief that the best managers seek to lead, through inspiration and example, and are not satisfied merely to exercise the authority that comes with their position. They believe it is the role of the leader to help their people develop professionally, to move out of their comfort zones and their well-know ways of getting things done into new patterns of operation and business behaviours. This includes adding skill sets and capabilities that go beyond the ways they complete tasks or write reports or talk with customers. I'm talking about achieving at a higher level in today's more complex business environment, and in understanding how to approach the issues of productivity, engagement and commitment. In order to raise the functional levels of their direct reports, managers must not only function fully within a new set of expanded boundaries but must also understand how to build and draw out these capabilities in their people.

As you look at your own organisations, I'm sure you can identify people in management positions whom you would classify as a leader. They are the people to whom others look for advice and whose opinions are valued across departments and teams. They may or may not manage groups of people, but they provide direction, inspiration, and vision. They are honest and authentic and they conduct themselves with integrity and sincerity. Their language and attitudes are positive and objective so you feel you can reasonably believe what they say — they are people you instinctively trust. You probably could name others who are "natural" leaders within the ranks of employees at all levels...again; those are the people to whom their peers look for thought leadership and who can be relied upon to objectively weigh the facts and circumstances when facing a decision. They help their fellows accept change and work easily with their superiors to make things happen. I'm sure you see the patterns of behaviour here. Leaders always operate at the Adult level and they exhibit the qualities of human beings who are interested in the wellbeing of others, in being fair and evenhanded, and in whom honesty and trustworthiness are ingrained characteristics.

While it is possible to find instances in history when "leaders" exhibited undesirable characteristics, let's not confuse charisma with leadership. These people have charisma, a trait that leaders also typically have, but it is one built on the ability to inspire fear and motivate people who are looking for ways to dominate and control others. There's also a significant similarity between those individuals: their success is fleeting and they eventually fail (are defeated, are overthrown — you get the picture). So don't confuse tyrants who wield power and are able to force or influence people to follow them with true leaders whose hearts and motives are for the good.

Not everyone is a born leader: it's a nature–nurture phenomenon. Some people grow up around people who provide excellent behavioural examples of leadership. They are able to observe leadership in action and it becomes instinctive to emulate that behaviour because they grow up seeing and experiencing the benefits inured from it to themselves and others. Other people inherently grow into adulthood with the capacity to inspire and motivate others — two critical behaviours exhibited by every leader. They are the children to whom others are drawn on the playground, whose lead the other children will follow for happy outcomes. And they mature into adults who are chosen, promoted and elected to positions of leadership in business, spiritual and community situations.

Now that we have identified leadership as an innate or ingrained ability to inspire others, what happens when individual contributors are promoted to management positions and they don't have the innate ability to inspire others to follow their lead? Do I think an individual can be taught to be a leader? Yes. Do I think those with an innate ability to inspire and motivate others have an advantage — of course. But there are great personal rewards for the individual who seeks to learn and practice the principles of leadership.

In fact, leadership training is an integral part of my business. I believe that fundamentally all people from whatever background or level of intelligence have untapped leadership potential. All most people need to develop their leadership a capability is really good coaching that comes out of an understanding of which habits to cultivate.

Whether through training programmes or coaching intervention, I usually work on Leadership development on both a transactional and emotional level. This requires that I SHOW people the skills of BEING a leader, and demonstrate pragmatically the key steps to follow. At the same time, there can't be a "one size fits all" approach, and leaders must understand the need for flexibility before they can lead. After all, the definition of a leader is someone who has followers. Whether your people are following you or not happens on an emotional rather than an intellectual level. (This happens in the same way empowerment does – people FEEL they want to follow.)

If leadership were something you could do on a transactional / task level — guided by a step by step instructional or operational manual — organisations would be run by computers and machines. Instead, capturing the emotional capacity of a leader is equally as important as understanding the tasks and transactions of a leader. An effective leader appreciates that all people are different, with their own unique characters, emotions and, well, DNA. Equally, an effective leader knows how to communicate to people on many levels, and also knows that a failure to do this will mean they are seen as a Parent.

My Leadership approach is based on a leadership triangle — Teacher, Values, Ideas.

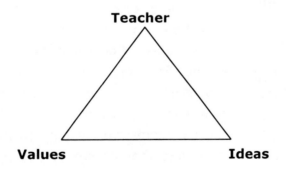

I work on the premise that Leaders are teachers; not in the academic, prescriptive way, but rather in an Adult-like Yoda / Guru way. Leaders have the ability to "teach" their own people how to display Lemon characteristics by modelling it themselves. They also have the ability to shape the mindset and the viewpoint of another individual through their positive influence. Leaders are teachers in that they can show the way. In fact, I often tell my clients that, "The ultimate measure of a great leader is that they develop a set of followers who are equipped to take over." True leaders have such an ability to teach that when the leader departs, one of the team takes over. In that sense, then, the pupil becomes the master.

For this reason, truly effective leaders (sustained by taking back the time the Monkey Syndrome stole from them) spend most of their time teaching — that is, coaching and developing people. Of course a leader drowning in Monkeys never has the time to teach and the negative behaviour they model for their direct reports trains the next generation of managers to repeat the cycle of the Monkey Syndrome.

I find that the most common mistake leaders make is thinking Leadership is all about transactions and tasks: creating and applying strategies, methodologies and tools. Instead, it's all about communication, thought, action, motivation and teaching.

An effective leader performs well because she backs up her words with actions, embodies her values and regularly challenges the validity of her actions based on her values.

Leaders are Lemons by another name and they are able to take their big ideas and act on them, thus they initiate action rather than wait passively for instructions on how to handle the action initiated from the ideas of others. Nor do they pass their ideas up the line for their managers to assume the responsibility. They act on their own ideas, turning them into a platform to raise their profiles and enabling themselves to become role models ... star performers that inspire others. It's for this reason that I often encourage my clients to undertake projects based on their big ideas. The irony is that by taking action on their leadership projects they are compelled to BE leaders to achieve them.

BEING a leader is a role to live up to, not a right to behave in a certain way. To be a leader, one must understand that what you do speaks far louder than what you say, so the concept that "actions speak louder" is a precept linked to the leader's values. Once again, the organisation's corporate/core values become a reference point for the leader's behaviour, and are almost more important than the traditional competency framework. A leader needs to have clear values and support them transparently with everything that she does. The leader embodies these values and models them by her own behaviour, thereby teaching and encouraging others to apply values to their own decision making and actions. An effective leader always performs better than an ineffective leader because she backs up her words with actions, she embodies her values in every way and she regularly challenges the validity of her actions based on her values. A good leader continuously challenges herself to truly lead with her values. An example of this would be a leader that, in teaching the value of teamwork and working with others to achieve results, passes the litmus test of being a team player. Neither is leadership about delegation or handing out a list of actions and expecting transformation and change. The old maxim: "you can't be a leader until you can lead yourself" rings true: you cannot expect someone to follow you if you do not, above all, do what you say you will do, as well as what your say others should do.

Effective leaders work hard at growing Lemons because they know that energy helps people overcome challenges and barriers, and its helps people to achieve stretch objectives. A good leader is never "Lemon-neutral" — they are either giving people the energy or they are using the energy from others for sustenance. To create positive Lemon behaviour in others the Leader must demonstrate zest and enthusiasm — it's contagious! They look for ways to improve the enthusiasm and zest levels of others at every turn, knowing that energy is the "fuel cell" of Lemons. Without that energy, direct reports can lose the FEELING of followership and dismiss the opportunity for empowerment that is being offered them. Equally, at an organisational or cultural level, good leaders know that once the "fuel cells" of their followers get low they risk the Monkeys coming back – it's a natural human reaction to resort to passing the Monkey when we feel low on zest.

Lessons Learned

Not every manager I work with has the potential to become a leader of Lemons, nor is that potential always obvious at first glance. Another great lesson involves a small owner-managed business. I was coaching the owner/manager, whom I will call Bill, who had a very prickly Parent personality and he was a big fan of titanic leaders in recent history. His emotional ownership attachment to the business was self-evident, and as a result, his people felt it difficult to outshine him, challenge him, or grow professionally and personally while working under him. Ironically, Bill wanted to sell the company and leave a legacy. He wanted the people he had put into management positions beneath him to lead the company, and even hoped one or two of them could be the new owners.

However, Bill was as arrogant as he was charismatic. He was a great sales person too: the reason the company had the financial value and performance it had was largely due to his initiative. If he were suddenly to get run over by a bus, the company would have gone bankrupt without his management.

It was obvious to me that there was a crying need to grow followers to ultimately take over so there would be leadership strength in the future. Bill was unable to "show the way," and he did not have the leadership skills to model Lemon characteristics or to teach any direct report to take over for him. Further, this was not happening from the bottom up because of a fear culture: no one wanted to challenge him, to attempt to rise to his level. I realised as I began working with Bill that none of his direct reports would ever be prepared to step up to the plate and raise their profile for fear of his criticism. He fed this fear by doing the usual Parental stuff to quell any Energy that built within his company.

Because Bill was the owner, as well as the key manager, he had no real reason to change. He also had no CEO or other senior manager to give him feedback and apply healthy pressure to encourage him to find a better way of managing and an effective way of leading. His historical passion for titanic leaders meant that his template for excellence was, in fact, Parental. He motivated like a military general. Bill would walk into the main open-plan office, give feedback out loud to someone or say something publicly critical, and then leave the room believing that it would motivate or inspire them. His internal arrogance, bullish ego and the fact that he had no real reason to change meant that Bill was **never going** to change – at least that's what most people thought.

The first thing I did was sack him! I told him not to come into the office for a whole week. He didn't. What happened that week was mixed and interesting. He came back to loads of emails — people communicated that way with him as it was less threatening. He also had a tonne of paperwork to sign off, as he wouldn't allow anyone else to deal with things. But at the same time, people reported to me that they felt, especially as the week went on, very much better without him in the office. The team worked closer together, they were forced to make some decisions and they managed their own people simply because they had to. By encouraging him to abandon his role he was able to see the net effects of his presence.

Here's what he found:

1. Morale and confidence was noticeably higher (especially as the week went on)

2. As we read each and every email and looked at each piece of paper, I challenged him to open his mind to what he was seeing. He realised that much of what he was wading through could have been dealt with by other people had he showed he had enough confidence in them that they could feel able to handle it.

I asked him, "How much time do you think you could create for yourself if you just let go?" Bill realised he had never considered this, and had no immediate answer.

Bill discovered his managers could make decisions if they were allowed to do so.

He realised that at the end of the week the company wasn't bankrupt — nothing major had happened — and without his influence his people weren't too afraid to take the initiative.

3. He was then encouraged to keep staying away – at least 2 days per week (he played golf).

When Bill came back from his one-week self-imposed "lay off," I had proven to him he wasn't needed. This was the cathartic process he had to experience to be able to let go of his Parental controlling attitudes and behaviours. We then worked on how best to spend his newly discovered time to BE a Leader not chief administrator. I showed him how to coach, how to pass on energy, and how to live his values and encourage others to embody theirs. And while it looked at first like he neither wanted nor was capable of changing and becoming a true Leader, he proved that with the right eye-opening experiences and some determination, he could become the first Lemon in his company — and allow his direct reports to become Lemons as well.

Making Sure New Managers Become Leaders

It's one thing to take existing managers and work with them to change their attitudes and behaviours — to make them into Lemons who Lead. However, a good number of managers are internally recruited from a junior position into a first line, first time management position. In order to get promoted in the first place, the new first time manager will have shown some degree of Lemon behaviour and responded to their own managers' style effectively; and even if the style they mirrored was their manager's Parental style — they must have done something right. It is most likely they will have shown energy, commitment, results, and confidence in order even to be considered for promotion. **BUT** when a person gets their first management position they can, and most often do, lapse into a Parental style – especially if it's a culturally significant style that is prevalent and supported within the organisation. Without specific training in how to be a manager, they mirror the management behaviour they have internalised ... from their parents and from managers under whom they worked in the past. They adopt the persona of someone with authority they have observed because they mistakenly believe that is how you lead people and achieve results.

Observing successful Parentally styled managers would be especially confusing if they work in a company where those behaviours and attitudes get positive attention. Whilst it's possible, before their promotion, to provide skills to a junior in how to manage and lead people, often the automatic instinct to display parental behaviour overrides any learning they may have experienced beforehand. Fundamentally, because until they actually have the title of manager, any training or development is hypothetical — even where they have been given pre-promotion responsibility. Based on what was internalised during childhood, the automatic reaction to instruct (give direction) via Tell and Do or to protect through nurturing gets the better of most people. The key point here is that new first time managers need to be mentored and coached to prevent them forming early habits that will be difficult to break later – or worse, early poor performance that will write off their chances before they've even had opportunity to get their new office chair warm.

Those organisations that have more natural Lemons than Monkeys do this well: they recruit from within and they manage continually to grow Lemons, even when their people are faced with new experiences or responsibilities. They provide leadership, coaching and training, both practical and intuitive, to ensure that the new manager understands what Lemon approach to management will be successful in the organisation, and that, although there could be examples of Parental Tell – Do attitudes living within for whatever reason, the star managers reject those and will model leadership actions and Lemon characteristics for their employees.

The organisations that do this badly are guilty of recruiting from within and not supporting the former Lemon or properly training the Lemon on the edge of Monkey behaviour. Where they fail is in allowing that person to revert to Monkey behaviour and move into a fully realised Monkey Syndrome. It's the perpetuation cycle – the root cause of most organisational Monkeys.

Zest and the High-Performing Employee

Let's go back to the Lemons. The point of the Lemon metaphor is to draw a sharp contrast between the business environment where both the manager and the direct report are living and working under the Monkey Syndrome and an environment that is filled with enthusiastic, high-achieving confident people. In organisations where Lemons abound, productivity is high and employees are engaged and committed. There is actually zest in the way these people approach their jobs. Their managers ensure they thoroughly understand their roles and how those roles contribute to the bottom-line of the organisation. The managers have plenty of time to handle their boss-generated and system-generated responsibilities and still focus on coaching and developing their people. And you know why this is the case: these managers have made sure they have the right people in the right jobs and then they have gotten out of the way to let them do the jobs they were hired to do. They don't need to practice Tell – Do management techniques because their direct reports are accustomed to handling issues as they come up, and when direct reports feel they need to get sign-off before initiating action, they know to bring both the issues and the solutions to their managers for quick approval. There are no queues outside the manager's office with people lined up to dump their monkeys and then wait to be told the next step they should take. In this organisation, managers focus on cultivating the creativity and responsibility of their people. Employees are proud of the contribution they make to the success of the organisation and they understand how their individual actions do that. They are able to take change in stride and look at is as an opportunity to grow and expand their capabilities. They get regular feedback from their manager on their performance. In this organisation of Lemons, managers don't hide behind a performance review timetables and they don't dread the sessions they need to have with their direct reports, because they assess progress and give feedback on an ongoing basis. In fact, feedback is a regular part of the dialogue between managers and direct reports in a Lemon-filled organisation. It is a crucial communication tool and ensures that employees stay in sync with the direction of the team and the organisation as a whole. Here, direct reports manage tasks and managers manage people — and organisations reward Lemons.

Cultivating Lemons

The switch from a Monkey-driven team to a team full of high-functioning Lemons isn't impossible, but it does take concentrated effort on the part of the manager. It's my contention that the manager is the lynchpin of the system of turning monkeys into Lemons. The switch involves the manager taking a hard look at what is and isn't working for her and what she currently is getting out of living under the Monkey Syndrome. Here are some concrete steps that will put zest into the organisation and make Lemons.

◆ The manager begins by reviewing past encounters and the behaviours that lead to her feeling of being overwhelmed by the tasks she has taken on for her direct reports, as well as her feeling that her team is dragging her down and taking up her valuable time with their petty annoyances and inability to handle adequately their areas of responsibility.

◆ The manager understands, at last, that the command and control, Tell – Do, Parental style doesn't work and only perpetuates the Child-like behaviour of her direct reports that has become so discouraging to her. She further realises that it is her willingness to Parent the monkeys of her direct reports that is causing part of the problem, and that it is tied up with her personal Parental style of management. She knows she can replace their need to get answers from her with their desire to show her how self-reliant and self-directed they can become by working with each one to distinguish and appreciate their own capabilities and the advantages to them of channelling their skills into performing at and above her expectations.

♦ Among the steps the manager resolves to take are to stop giving answers and taking on tasks, and to start encouraging — and even demanding — her direct reports come to her with solutions rather than problems. She finally understands she can get out of the Monkey Syndrome by letting her direct reports do their jobs. And while she may have to reassess the skill levels of some people, she has the opportunity to set up those that need to focus on different areas of responsibility for more successful outcomes.

♦ The manager also resolves to change her vocabulary, leaving behind the judgmental, critical words and patronising language. She sees that this is a very visible sign to her direct reports of the changes she is making in her own management style.

♦ She focuses on the crucial aspects of managing the performance of her team by helping them set SMART objectives. (SMART objectives are Specific, Measurable, Achievable, Relevant and Time-related.)

♦ She understands that Adults spend a lot of time coaching, while Parents instruct, direct and prescribe. She recognises the habits she has fallen back on in the past (the Monkey Syndrome habits) and resolves to concentrate her efforts on identifying and providing for the coaching and developmental needs of her team.

♦ She decides to go beyond the set performance management timetable and create frequent and meaningful opportunities for giving feedback, on both the task accomplishment and the behaviour, of her direct reports. The appraisal process for her team is repositioned into an opportunity for dialogue and a powerful process to help employees move their careers and their capabilities to the next level. Whatever the negative connotations that might have been put on the appraisal process in the past, the manager is able, by her behaviour, to change it into a highly creative and positive chance to create frequent dialogue and support. This doesn't mean that problems are glossed-over or behaviour issues are swept under the rung, but by using an Adult approach to identifying and working on problems, the manager can set up the situation with each direct report to work on them in a positive and constructive way.

◆ While she can choose to abandon the Parent role, she realises that it will take a lot of work on her part to help those on her team who have fallen into the Child role to move out of it and adopt Adult behaviours.

◆ She understands that each direct report needs clear direction as well as direct feedback. The rules of the game can't be changed to meet any outside agendas ... expectations must be set up front and must be fair for everyone.

◆ The manager recognises her role as communicator for her team. Communication isn't about giving orders or instructions, it's about dialogue and understanding, and articulating behaviours, attitudes, objectives and objectives that set up the direct report for success. She knows that when they win, she wins; they understand that the success of the team is enhanced by their personal success, and vice versa. She also understands how important it is to create dialogue about the business objectives of the organisation and ensure that each of her team members has a line of sight between what they do in and the objectives of the organisation.

Key Points Summary

♦ While the Monkey Syndrome wastes managers' time and promotes a Parental management style, growing Lemons does the opposite: Lemons are the zest of the organisation, infusing it with energy, enthusiasm, confidence, willingness to learn, readiness for action and a positive approach to business.

♦ Managers/leaders who cultivate Lemons do so with a strategy for empowerment that is consistently applied.

♦ Managers of Lemons are successful Lemons themselves and serve as inspiring role models for Lemon behaviour.

♦ Lemons make decisions and take action within the areas in which they are empowered.

♦ Interacting within the Adult style promotes productivity and grows Lemons.

♦ The Adult management style frees the manager from time-wasting tasks that rightfully belong to her direct reports.

♦ The Adult management style enables the manager to focus on both his own duties and responsibilities to his boss and the system and at the same time direct his energies into the development of his people.

♦ The "voice of authority" that comes out in Parent mode is an ingrained perspective based on the childhood experiences of the manager. The way it manifests depends greatly on the behaviours those experiences contain.

♦ Communication between people in all parallel modes except Adult – Adult is more fluid and comfortable but non-productive because neither the Child nor the Parent will be able to effectively create a meaningful solution by themselves.

- Managing is about exercising authority. Leading is about inspiring and motivating.

- Leaders are born with an innate ability to inspire and motivate. Leadership can also be taught to those who desire to focus their personal positive motivations in a way that inspires others to adopt the same thought process and practice.

- A manager's focus on coaching and performance feedback is the cornerstone of Adult management behaviour and the lynchpin of cultivating Lemons.

- Switching from monkey behaviour to Lemons is achieved through concentrated effort by the manager to identify and change behaviours that play into the Monkey Syndrome.

Managing Performance

PERFORMANCE MANAGEMENT SUCCESS RELIES ON MATCHING WHAT IS MEANINGFUL TO THE EMPLOYEE WITH WHAT SUPPORTS THE OBJECTIVES OF THE ORGANISATION

Company Policies and Competency Models

It has been the practice of all larger organisations, and many mid-size or smaller as well, to establish company policies and programmes against which to measure the performance and growth of their employees. There are levels of complexity that range from straight employee assessment against management-defined expectations to 360-degree feedback programmes that strive to look at performance from peer and direct report perspectives, as well as through the eyes of the superior. Defining clear expectations is probably one of the hardest aspects of all because it takes a conscientious manager and an engaged employee to work together to define SMART objectives (see Chapter 4). The next most difficult aspect is ensuring that a company performance management discussion is not a once-a-year event. That practice is all too often the approach taken by managers, however well-intentioned, and employees who don't realise or believe they have a responsibility to initiate performance discussions with their superiors. Finally, the end cap to performance management difficulties is keeping personalities out of the process: this means the personalities of the employee whose performance is being reviewed, the manager doing the review, and the influence of others outside the process. It is a fine line between taking objective input from others in the organisation and listening and giving credence to the sour- grapes Child behaviour of employees with a grudge. Add to that the Monkey Syndrome and you have a recipe for frustration and worthless activity. Theoretically a company will create performance management policies and programmes as a way to measure and reward performance, keep productivity high and achieve organisational results. In a practical sense, it often turns out to be a frustrating exercise in paper-pushing and conflict-avoidance for poorly trained managers, and feelings of reliving the Spanish Inquisition for employees. A performance review is one of the quickest avenues to Parent—Child behaviour-land I can think of, where it seems impossible to separate the individual from the performance. Many parents have trouble being able to correct behaviour while, at the same time, maintaining their child's self-esteem. "I don't approve of what you did" too often is translated as "I don't approve of/like/love you" by a submissive child and results in demoralisation for the child and either aggravation or remorse for the parent. It doesn't work in a real life parent—child relationship, and it certainly doesn't work in business, where managers shouldn't be acting like parents anyway and the Parent-Child mode of interaction is destructive and illogical. Performance Management handled in this fashion insures that Lemons are never cultivated and the Monkey Syndrome reigns supreme. However, in a Lemon-filled company where managers operate as Adults and the Monkey Syndrome is under control, using performance management programmes and thoughtfully-developed and specifically assigned competencies fertilises their Lemons ... brings out the best in the workforce ... because performance management is a tool in the hands of the right people.

The tendency to slip into Parent mode and use performance management processes as a method for controlling the behaviour of employees by using parental correction techniques can be very tempting for managers who aren't operating from their Adult perspectives. How easy it is for managers in the throes of the Monkey Syndrome to ignore or avoid opportunities to set employees on the right track by spending meaningful time with them to objectively look at attitudes, behaviours and results and help them come up with alternative ways of working. After all, they are buried in monkey chaos and can't see above what is piled on their desks. Couple this with the resentment that builds knowing they are spending so much time cleaning up monkey messes that they have no time to fulfil their boss or organisation imposed responsibilities, and you find managers who are unable to see what is breaking down or holding back the potential greatness of their team.

In organisations where Lemons abound and interaction is guided by Adult to Adult behaviours, a well conceived and thoroughly integrated Performance

Management system is an exceptional way to guide and coach your employees to exceed performance expectations and feel fulfilled and confident in their positions.

Some companies have turned to competency models as a way to mitigate against the inadequacies of their performance management programmes, thinking that adding a layer of measurements will give managers something more to work with. Actually, the opposite is true because these are just sticking plasters for a gaping wound. If your performance management programme isn't helping managers to objectively and accurately analyse the performance of their direct reports it is likely that either they weren't trained thoroughly enough to use the tools effectively or they aren't being held accountable for following the programme guidelines. There is also a possibility that the performance management system in place is not designed to effectively yield the desired results. I'm not saying I am against competency models; on the contrary, they can be exceedingly positive tools to identify the desired skills, traits, and talents an organisation needs to achieve a competitive advantage in the market place. My problem with them is that when they are used in the wrong way or in the wrong hands, they become another layer of inappropriate positional requirements where the competencies serve primarily as a lever to prove how ineffectively an employee is performing rather than as a guide to ensure that the right people are in the right jobs with the guidance and support they need to be successful.

Competencies should be used to define behaviour patterns, skill sets, innate abilities and the traditional knowledge bases of workers and managers.

While I caution my clients against throwing competency models on top of broken performance management programmes, I believe that well-developed competency models actually can be exceedingly beneficial if they are used to identify the critical success factors for individuals in specific positions. Competencies have been variously defined by experts in the field of performance management, but the key concepts for me are the ways in which they can be used to define behaviour patterns, skill sets, innate abilities and the traditional knowledge bases of workers and managers within Lemon cultures. Competency definitions need to include the intellectual and interpersonal abilities necessary to perform with confidence, commitment and enthusiasm. They have been generalised by many into a set of descriptions that are so diluted and non-specific that they can fit anyone in any situation. As I've said earlier in this book, it's not a one-size-fits-all world, so competencies, to have any hope of affecting positive improvements within an organisation and identifying the high-performing Lemons, must be specific on one level to the position, but on another level to the individual. Having a generic competency model that may change by a few words from department to department within the company does little more than add another layer of complexity to an already shaky performance management process. It would be like dressing triplets alike for their whole lives ... eventually they will become frustrated, irritated and demotivated without recognition of their own individuality. Put another way, a competency model will have positive impact for an organisation full of Lemons if it combines characteristics such as the traits, skills, knowledge, behaviour patterns, values, and motives that apply to both distinct work areas within an organisation and, on a very specific level, to the individual within their performance plan.

Managing Against Meaningful Objectives. The concept of managing performance by establishing and working toward the achievement of objectives was introduced in the mid-1950s and has been used in performance appraisal and review practices in various forms since then. The concept pre-dates many contemporary performance management processes and seems to have become embedded in one way or another in most of them. In theory it is an excellent way to make sure that the activities against which the employee is being measured have some meaning to the organisation and achieve results that relate to the mission of the company. The problem I have seen in practice in organisations that are overrun by the Monkey Syndrome is that many times managers fail to help the employee match organisationally meaningful objectives with ones that support their own internal motivations and professional objectives. This breaks down the review process because it depersonalises the whole experience for the employee. It is compounded by the poorly operating manager in full Monkey mode because the initiative for employees to achieve at even their basic required job duties has been usurped, let alone to accomplish any stretch objectives the employee might have wanted to set for the purpose of expanding her professional skill sets. As we've seen, the manager embroiled in the Monkey Syndrome has no time for discussions with his direct reports on their professional objectives or company-directed objectives, being too busy taking care of all the monkeys screaming for attention. What happens, as the manager becomes more and more ineffective, is that the employee is driven further and further from professional opportunities as well as any chance to excel in ways that have a direct, positive impact on organisational success. This is further compounded by the dismal experiences that are inevitably a part of the performance review process, conducted in Parent mode. I have so often heard from managers that these are the interviews that they most dread because it is in these situations that they must be "brutally honest" with their employees and show them just how disappointing their performance has been for the team and the organisation. (See any Adults in this scenario? I thought not.) Employees, likewise, express dread and anxiety expecting a continuation of the Tell and Do behaviours with which they have become so familiar. They see these encounters as anything but positive and seek to cast as small a shadow as possible during the interview. This is definitely not any type of communication ... it is a Parent to Child behaviour modification session. No good can come of this for either party. These anxiety ridden sessions are not only personally discouraging and departmentally useless, but they are also organisationally worthless because they do nothing to cultivate Lemons ... committed, skilled, confident workers. There is no objective identification of growth opportunities for the employee, and the manager reinforces his own negative Parent-oriented behaviour by focusing on **telling** the direct report what she has done wrong. Notwithstanding the fact that most humans learn best from their mistakes, the Parent mode in business is not conducive to constructive interpretation by the employee of how to modify their approaches, attitudes or tactics in the future in ways that will be successful, because Tell-Do Parent techniques do not provide a sufficient learning opportunity for an adult in which the individual can determine for herself, with guidance, the actions that will be successful. Rather, in Parent mode, the manager is correcting and directing the actions of the direct report, which to be effective, nearly always requires that the direct report **stop thinking** about it and just act as directed.

Part of what is wrong in how companies approach their performance management processes is that the set up, while possibly by the book, is wrong and sets the stage for these inquisition style Parent to Child encounters. Here are typical performance management process steps:

- Manager presents the job description and performance evaluation sheet to the employee

- Manager sets quantifiable performance targets and subjective behaviour targets

- Manager picks a date for an interim progress assessment (which often never occurs because the manager is too busy caring for monkeys)

- Manager writes up the assessment and notifies the employee when to show up (in some circumstances the employee may be charged with seeking a meeting, presenting another way in which he may "get it wrong" when he has serious difficulties pinning down the over-Monkeyed manager's schedule)

- Manager gives the employee the written and verbal assessment.

What is wrong with this procedure, you ask? What is wrong is that it's all about the manager. It's the manager's responsibility and the manager's decisions about the employee's performance that drive everything. This process is not about engaging the employee in defining objectives that are meaningful personally as well as organisationally; nor is it remotely about communicating the progress the employee makes toward her objective achievement throughout the year. Further, the manager is too busy wrangling Monkeys to even notice what the employee is doing, never mind how well she is doing it. On the other hand, the employee isn't remotely engaged in this process because it has been dictated and it ignores any professional growth objectives she may have. By the time the mid-year arrives without any meaningful discussion between the employee and the manager, both are afraid to talk about what is going on. The employee practices avoidance because she doesn't want to hear what is wrong with her until she has to do so; the manager, likewise, practices avoidance because she doesn't have time to think about how the team is working or pay attention to what this employee is doing. By the end of the year, they are in a hopeless quagmire of mis-conception and mis-information. It turns into a numbers game, because in the end, in most cases, the manager must assign some numerical assessment of the employee's performance for the purposes of record-keeping and pay adjustment. Not only does this not exhibit the contribution this employee may or may not have made to the productivity and success of the organisation, it has only the most surface analysis contained in a harried last minute write-up based more on the performance of the team under the manager's direction than the actual performance of the individual. It exemplifies the typically poor Monkey Syndrome-driven performance of the manager, and it certainly does not reflect any actual analysis of the achievements and competencies of the employee. Once again, the Monkey Syndrome creates havoc in the manager's pursuit of performance management, subverts the direct report's chance of demonstrating his capabilities, and totally eliminates any meaningful communication between the manager and direct report. Take the case of manager McHugh, who works in a complex organisation full of various management practices, including an intricately formal performance management process.

> McHugh is a seasoned, over-burdened manager with a difficult job made more difficult by his inability to distinguish between issues brought to him by his direct reports in which he needs to personally become involved and issues that he should push back to them. McHugh typically has an office stacked to the ears with folders, project timelines, and blueprints, few of which has he had the time to look over, much less take action upon. McHugh is basically a "good guy" with every intention of doing right by his team. His intentions most often hover in the upper reaches of his office, caught in a perpetual game of toss by the Monkeys that run riot

on his desk. While his organisation has rather rigid strictures governing their performance review policies, in actual practice the General Manager sets the pace by being chronically late conducting his reviews, which, in effect, stamps "OK to Delay" on the minds of all but the most personally driven managers within his division. Coupled with the fact that a poor job was done in orienting managers to a new system instituted but two years previously, this performance management programme has little chance of accomplishing any positive objectives toward creating a competitive advantage for the company through cultivating employee excellence. As McHugh turns the page in his desk calendar he realises with a start that his fiscal year-end reviews are due in 4 days time, and he has not had even the briefest of communication with some of his direct reports about their objectives, performance or what extra projects or activities have been added to their list of job responsibilities during the year. Deciding he has to put the monkeys in a cage for a few minutes, McHugh jots off emails to his direct reports assigning them dates and times to meet individually in his office for what he jokingly labels their annual scourging. McHugh is showing very clearly that he does not value the programme by acting at what is obviously the last minute, by demanding their presence at a prescribed time and place without regard for their individual schedules, and by creating the aura of predetermined disapproval by labeling the process in the most onerous of terms. McHugh and his direct reports have little chance of coming out of these pending encounters with anything constructive. McHugh has set himself up as judge, jury and executioner in a court of professional scrutiny. His direct reports have 4 days in which their dread can build to a fevered pitch, throwing themselves into a period of panic during which little productive results can be accomplished for themselves or their team.

Performance management programmes so often don't work because everyone is afraid of the process, and no true communication occurs at any point along the time line. In no way should a performance management programme be conducted as a punitive, retribution-filled exercise, nor should it be allowed to become a numbers game. If it devolves to either of those, a company is better off abandoning formal performance management processes altogether because this kind of behaviour does more damage than it does good. The case of manager McHugh is a classic one in which the Monkey Syndrome so controls the time and attention of the manager that he is paralysed in his efforts to manage his people. McHugh will rely on an analytical rehash of the achievement percentile of his direct reports and cover any personal attitudes or job-oriented infractions, with no time, information or inclination to look at the individual's objectives or professional aspirations, alignment with company objectives or accomplishments outside the fixed parameters of the performance criteria set in the previous January. At best, a high-performing employee might come out fine with the numbers test, assuming nothing out of the ordinary came up to which his priorities were shifted. Other employees with excellent potential, but who need guidance and direction to mature in various aspects of their positions, will doubtless come out on the short end because they have experienced McHugh as the Parent all year, because they have been unable or too afraid to take the initiative in any situation, and because their activities and duties have been controlled without consideration for their strengths or areas where they need coaching or training. As for McHugh, his week will be full of dread for the difficult position he is in ... having to "set many people straight" on their failings. He will look for excuses to put off writing his reviews because he is ill-prepared to analyse the performance of his direct reports and because he really doesn't have the time to take his attention from the 60 screaming, chattering Monkeys that are camped out in all corners of his office. His resentment will build from his own subconscious feelings of being inadequately prepared to analyse and write his reviews, his stress level, his sense that employees are fearful, and his lack of time. And where do the objectives factor into all of this? They went right out the window the minute they were put to paper ... if they ever were put to paper. If objectives were recorded, given this manager's propensity to be embroiled in the Monkey Syndrome — which means he has usurped his direct reports' opportunities to care for their own Monkeys and perform at or above an acceptable level — they likely bare little resemblance to what this team has been able to accomplish during the year or to what would be meaningful personally to each individual's career growth. This department, when looked at objectively, is a typical Tell and Do environment: department performance is driven not by employees acting on and fulfilling their performance targets but rather by the direction and demands of the manager who makes all decisions and tells direct reports at all levels what to do next. His overwork (by now he is barely able to drag himself from his car to the office because of the weight of all the Monkeys who accompany him everywhere) is reflected in his slow responses and the roadblocks he creates when his entire team has to look for his direction and approval of every action and every decision. Equally, the manager doesn't have the training or capacity to embrace a rather rigid performance management programme. The company practice of giving the programme little respect or attention (as embodied in the General Manager's behaviour) leads to a breakdown in the efficacy of the process; and no one benefits from the resultant mis-direction, anxiety and emotional stress.

Lessons Learned

Hilary was a Departmental Head for a large national business and was responsible for nearly 100 people. She also had 6 people reporting directly to her. I became aware of her lack of enthusiasm for Performance Management after running a couple of workshops for the wider business, which a few of her direct reports attended. In the workshops, her people were complaining about their recent mid-year reviews to other members of the group. Indeed, throughout the workshop other pieces of information came to light regarding her overall management style – illustrating that her style was very Tell and Do oriented. I met Hilary a few weeks later during a meeting on team and employee development. During the meeting, as we were discussing the need to conduct meaningful performance management sessions with her team, her body language clearly pointed out her attitude: she scowled and claimed that such matters were a waste of time – following this up with the statement that she didn't have the time to do them anyway. However, in the next breath she complained that her team were not raising their profile or stepping up to the plate – their apparent unwillingness to take on responsibility was clearly annoying to her. A few weeks before I had heard from members of her team that her review meetings were one-way conversations, which she rushed through, and were marked by a mutual unease of the whole process. She had reduced most of the review to a meagre one page document that prescribed her opinions and remedies. She spent the entire twenty minute meeting going through the points she had pre-written one by one. Furthermore, the tension, stress and apprehension that permeated the team descended upon those that had yet to experience the process. They had heard how the performance management sessions were conducted from those who went before, and they were waiting in fear of their own meeting with Hilary knowing that they would meet with the same fate.

Hilary and here team were trapped in the all too common malaise of seeing the whole performance management process as a painful paper exercise designed by those anal 'box-tickers' in HR. After all, according to Hilary and other like-minded managers, the only reason why we have performance reviews is to justify pay increases.

Hilary, meanwhile, was oblivious to the truth. If only she knew what her team thought of her and her approach to the performance management process. If only she knew the effect that her overall management style had on the team atmosphere and their likely individual development curves. What would she think and do?

Two weeks after my encounter with Hilary, I met again with her team members. They had little idea of what to do next or how to accomplish the nebulous improvements she had asked for. As I looked around the room I realised that, furthermore, they looked utterly confused about the entire process and abused by the direction they were receiving.

As I reflected on the situation with Hilary and her team, I knew this was a position in which many, many teams and organisations found themselves, and I also knew that it required a paradigm shift to effect change in these circumstances. The paradigm to which I refer is one based on the opinion that performance management programs are useless HR exercises designed to create a file document that will justify salary and personnel actions. It takes a drastic change in those basic assumptions about the purpose and process of performance management to reverse the spiral effect that this common paradigm creates. In this case, both the team members and Hilary had to change. Whilst she had created the current paradigm through her own beliefs and attitudes, Hilary could not, now, reverse this on her own — it was too deeply rooted in the dysfunction of her team. Hilary and her team had a lot of work to do together to make the necessary paradigm shift into a healthy performance management environment.

First, it would take a shift from Hilary to realise that what she was doing was, in fact, the very reason why she had no time; and that it was also the very reason why the team lacked initiative and was unable to take responsibility.

Second, the team needed to understand how to participate properly in performance management reviews.

Unfortunately, the ending of this story is not a satisfying one. Hilary chose not to look closely at her own behaviour or consider the consequences of her management style. She is still at the company, in the same role and is behaving with the same disdainful attitude toward her company's performance management programme. While she reluctantly admits she is somewhat more aware of her actions, she refuses to change either her attitudes and beliefs or her actions. Her employees are still fearful, anxious and frustrated, and continue to look upon performance management discussions with Hilary as a torture session. Unfortunately, Hilary came by her management style the way many misguided managers do ... she learned it from her own Director who has, and still is, committing similar "crimes" against performance management. Her Director has allowed her, and truth be told, has encouraged her, to continue her behaviours and attitudes for 10 years. She has not been able to grow professionally, nor have her direct reports. If she maintains her vigilant stance against change and compliance with the performance management policy, she faces the possibility of being thrust out of the company in a redundancy sweep.

Using Competencies to Lemon-ise Your Team. In a Lemon-filled organisation, adding competencies for specific jobs and individuals provides clarity around performance expectations, and is a roadmap for future professional development. Competencies should never be so generalised that they fit any and all departments, regardless of their business focus. For example, members of the Customer Service Department have some obviously critical necessary competencies that will ensure customer's are treated with respect and courtesy, and excellent customer service representatives will embody certain personal characteristics that enable them to be extremely competent in dealing with the public. These characteristics include, for example, patience, a friendly approach to strangers, being slow to anger, and an ability to depersonalise the conversation and maintain a professional approach in the face of customer irritation or abuse, as well as an ability to write notes, read a computer screen and speak English clearly, all at the same time. On the other hand, the engineering department staff have other unique competencies that will enable them to meet and exceed technology development objectives; such as, tenacity, creativity, logical/methodical thinking and a peculiar ability to deal with mathematical constructs. These two departments, while they are both striving to support organisational policies and contribute to the company mission, have distinctly different ways in which they do both. Although it would be easy to generalise these two sets of competencies into one generic statement that employees should demonstrate patience, professionalism, creativity and mature thinking, it would do a great disservice to both departments and the potential growth and Lemon success they could represent within the company to dilute the unique character of the competencies that could mark a competitive advantage demonstrated by each department's employees. All too often I have seen companies spend hours hammering out a set of competencies for one department, and then short-sightedly slot the same competencies with a few minor adjustments into every other department, thinking that if they reflect the business direction of the organisation they will be on target. The fallacy in that thinking is they are not giving credence to the distinctive way in which each department's role contributes to the success of the organisation as a whole. Customer service and product development each embody unique critical success factors that support the mission of the company, but the way in which they execute their duties and responsibilities is drastically different. You wouldn't want engineers to focus on core competencies that omit the analytical thinking that is critical to technical development; nor would you want customer service representatives to have patience and professionalism without the ability to multi-task while they are on the phone. The point of this comparison is to underscore the value of individualising competencies to a department's or team's role within the organisation. I believe it is even more useful to look at competencies for each individual, from both the perspective of their departmental roles and responsibilities, as well as from their individual strengths and opportunities for improvement. The issue, here, is that organisations must really analyse and understand what it will take for each department and team to deliver the optimum in performance. This is neither easy nor fast ... to develop meaningful department-specific competencies it takes the knowledge of a performance management professional in partnership with someone who has a depth and breadth of understanding of the business imperatives and bottom-line success factors of the company and of each department.

The Discipline of Performance Management

It's true: relevant performance management programmes that serve an organisation as both a compass and roadmap to excellence require managers to believe in them and to accept the responsibility to exercise the discipline required to make them work. I believe it has to begin at the top. A Managing Director who disregards the guidelines of the company's performance management system sets the pace. It is his practice of negligence and his cavalier attitude about the "rules of the game" that can make or break a performance management programme. Here are the principles I work with my clients to adopt when they set up an initial performance management programme or attempt to resurrect one that has broken down out of neglect and misuse.

> **Principle 1: Lead by example.** People watch what their leaders do far more than they listen to what they say. The Parental "do it because I said so" never works in family life (unless the Parent is ruling the family as a

dictator), and it stands no better chance of inspiring desired behaviour among operations managers in a business environment. Starting with the Managing Director, managers at all levels within the organisation must abide by the guidelines of the programme, including timing, communication and intent.

Principle 2: Train everyone and make it mandatory. There is no point in creating a performance management system that no one understands. The organisation must support the time factor, and yes, it will take away from day-to-day operations in a minimal way. But this far outweighs the potential benefits that a well-executed, ongoing programme brings to a company. All managers must be asked to devote adequate time to training sessions in order to become comfortable and knowledgeable about the process. This can't be done half way: some cannot be allowed to opt out, and upper level managers cannot be permitted to apply pressure to their managerial direct reports to avoid training for any reason. This will be particularly troublesome for managers with the Monkey Syndrome, because finding time to do anything other than wrangle monkeys will be nearly impossible for them. These managers are the worst at absorbing the intent and attitudes of good leaders who conscientiously work with their direct reports to identify and coach them on their key performance factors. This situation is made worse by their overburdened schedules that prevent any meaningful communication throughout the year, ensuring that their performance discussions are uncomfortable surprises.

It will take a financial commitment on the part of the company to support the training resources (people, location, materials) necessary to ground

> **Principles of Performance Management:**
>
> **1. Lead by example**
>
> **2. Train everyone**
>
> **3. Build in communication, day one**
>
> **4. Publicise and demand adherence to timetable**
>
> **5. Reviews done by Adults**

managers in the steps and responsibilities. Further, employees are no less in need of training than their managers. Employees must understand their responsibilities in the performance management process and be prepared to participate fully with their managers in establishing their performance criteria. Indeed, if employees are not an integral part of creating their objectives and performance targets, and identifying the measurements that will be used to assess their performance and development, it will all be a useless exercise. This can't be done in the Parent — Child mode; if it is, it is a waste of time because the employee won't be invested in the outcome. He will certainly have something at stake, but this is the kind of stakes where the employee ends up spending the year in confusion and apprehension. Equally concerning is that there will be no incentive to stretch toward a higher level of performance ... nothing in it for him other than a check mark in the right box and a rating number at the end. This type of performance management has many more negative consequences for the manager ... who has set himself up to carry the Monkeys all year... and for the direct report, who will continue to feel dictated to and dis-empowered. This is a no-win situation all around.

Principle 3: Build in communication from day one. There is no appraisal process that has ever been created that has a ghost of a chance of working well without thoughtful, consistent communication between manager and employee. I'm not speaking about thoughtful communication in the sense of it being kind or caring, though there is nothing wrong with that; I am specifically referring to a method of communication that is based on astute observation and careful consideration of the skills and behaviours, and yes, competencies, demonstrated by the employee. And this certainly is not intended to ensure that every infraction of the rules or misstep by the employee is highlighted. Performance-focussed communication is balanced; it praises as well as guides, and it is genuine, open and clear. Too many managers save all their comments about an employee's performance until the final performance review at the end of the year. It is, in fact, at that point too late to tell the employee much of anything; it's certainly too late to encourage her to continue good work, attitudes or skill development. It is equally too late to modify or improve any behaviours, attitudes or work habits that are not in line with the objectives of the individual and the organisation.

Communication is a skill that is not particularly inherent in managers: most need training and coaching to become capable communicators. Many managers do not take the time or apply the effort necessary to be comfortable communicating in-person or to be adept at communicating in writing. Such situations are a failing of Monkey Syndrome organisations and sometimes even of Lemon-rich ones. In fact, authentic communication mastery is one of the core competencies that should be front and centre in every manager's performance plan. For many, it will present a growth opportunity and a challenge, but to be a capable manager having the skill to communicate openly, unemotionally and clearly is as essential as having the commitment to communicate consistently and continuously. This isn't something that can be dismissed as unnecessary when a candidate is being considered for promotion into a management position. Wise organisations begin creating competency requirements within their managers' performance management plans before they tackle everyone else, because the core of management competency is communication.

Principle 4: Publicise and demand adherence to the performance management timetable. Create a manageable timetable for each step of the performance management process. Manageable is the key here ... don't expect managers to be able to handle this at peak business periods when they and their direct reports are stretched to the limit of their capacities. Set timing that is within reasonable parameters given market conditions, holidays, peak periods and anything else that affects your company's business cycle.

Then hold everyone to it. Unless there is an illness, accident, or severe business crisis that makes it humanly impossible for a manager to meet performance management timing, every manager should be held accountable if he does not communicate and meet with his direct reports to review their performance plans according to the schedule. There must be consequences for not following the schedule, and there should be rewards for successfully doing so. This does not speak to the quality of the review ... that's for Principle 5. What it does is place the management responsibility squarely where it belongs and ensures that if the requirements are not met, there are consequences for the manager that do not negatively impact the employee.

Conversely, the employee should have a role in keeping the process flowing so he is likewise invested in a cooperative venture with the manager. Good performance management programmes include self-review on some periodic basis, culminating at year end in a comprehensive analysis of all aspects of the individual performance plan. 360-degree feedback programmes also include reviews of and by peers and superiors. Each employee should be held accountable in their own performance plan for timely participation, or the entire process will yield none of the results for which it was established. Adherence to the timing seems like a rigid tactic, but it is absolutely essential if the whole structure of the performance management system is to be kept functioning. No system will be in the least effective if it isn't carried out according to the parameters created around it by the company. It can still fail if it isn't well-conceived and employee-centric, but there is **no** hope of success if it is done in a haphazard fashion.

Principle 5: Performance reviews must be done by Adults. The quality of a performance review is the real sticking point for many failed performance management programmes. Too often the manager is living the Monkey Syndrome and operating 90 percent of the time from his Parent perspective. This is why programmes break down ... they morph into Parental instruction sessions with no meaningful task or behaviour feedback coming from the manager. Done at the end of the performance review period with no communication during the intervening time, the Parent will point out everything that the direct report has failed on, and gloss over those areas that need improvement with little attention to the circumstances that have altered, as they always do, the employee's direction during that year. The manager in Adult mode, on the other hand, who has set up frequent, consistent opportunities to praise his direct report or guide, teach and coach him in more effective ways of handling situations and tasks throughout the year, will be able to approach the year-end review as a summary and recap of what has been discussed before. This will prevent unpleasant surprises, the embarrassing or irritating reactions of employees who are hearing the "bad news" for the first time, and feelings of betrayal and unfair treatment on the part of the employee. With good, consistent communication, the annual review is a chance to focus on what worked throughout the year and on what focal areas the employee wants/needs to concentrate to promote their capabilities and skills to the next level.

I use these principles as guidelines to layer on top of the official company performance management programme provisions. They apply to any type of performance management system and are universally successful when followed with serious intent and consistency. In my consultancy, I see many legacy programmes that may be out of date with current practice, but that can still evolve into effective performance management tools that serve the needs of the organisation. Typically, the older approaches are less complex and more straight-forward than are some of the ones in practice today. However, with adherence to the **5 Principles,** and application of the Appraisal Tips discussed in the next chapter, even a simple programme can be useful in the right hands. Lemon organisations will find this very consistent with the way they do business for it is the simple exercise of essential Lemon behaviours that guide much of their success:

- ◆ Lead from the top

- ◆ Train appropriately

- ◆ Communicate effectively

- ◆ Stick to the time table

- ◆ Operate on an Adult level

360-Degree Reviews

Part of performance appraisal is giving feedback to the individual. In traditional performance management systems, the bulk of the feedback comes from the manager, and certainly the manager is, or should be, in a position to view, review and assess the skills and qualities possessed by the people for whom she is responsible. I have encountered systems, particularly in organisations where there is a matrix management structure, where the manager giving a performance review doesn't actually have direct and frequent contact with the individual. That is a recipe for disaster and a discussion in itself. For now, suffice it to say, the only effective performance management system prescribes reviews that are done by managers who have direct responsibility and consistent, if not daily, interaction with the person receiving the review.

However, to get the most out of a performance review process, an individual needs to understand his strengths and weaknesses from the perspective of his peers and clients/customers as well. Although the origination of a 360-degree feedback process dates back to the 1940s, it has only fairly recently gained any appreciable level of understanding and acceptance. Recognition of the value of this multi-faceted review of employee performance has occurred in many ways as a response to the ability of technology to simplify and streamline the process of giving feedback ... as a result of the proliferation of Internet-based automated systems which provide access to the process for employees, managers and outside stakeholders around the world. Accommodating the language and timing needs of a wide-spread base of reviewers takes care of much of the hesitation employers have about including 360-degree feedback in their performance management systems. And let's be abundantly clear about this: 360 feedback is just that — feedback: it does not **become** the performance management system; it is just a tool among other important steps in the process. Simpler performance management programmes may be quicker and easier for managers to get through, but where there are simpler measures and fewer dimensions against which to assess, and where the input is limited to the opinions of the manager, the resulting appraisal is narrower, less balanced and less useful to the growth and career progression of the individual. While I believe strongly that the role of 360's is a significant part of the performance management success seen in Lemon organisations, I also believe that, in the wrong hands, it can do far more harm than good.

Here's how a 360-degree feedback process should work.

♦ Between 5 and 10 people should be asked to provide feedback, made up of peers, colleagues, customers/clients, if appropriate, and other supervisors and managers outside of the individual's direct reporting relationship. All reviewers should have consistent and fairly frequent interaction with the person for whom they are giving feedback. Once a year or rare contact, for example, will do nothing to enhance understanding of how their performance does or does not reflect the qualities and skills that are their critical success factors.

♦ The use of 360-degree feedback should become an integral part of the performance management system, not a one-off, occasional tactic. 360 feedback done on a haphazard frequency, or used by some managers on a discretionary basis, will have very negative effects on the morale and performance of employees.

♦ The feedback instrument should be written so it is clearly focussed on assessing observable behaviours, and should refrain from including any value judgments or insubstantial opinions.

♦ Everyone within an organisation needs training in how to give feedback, not just managers. To be useful at all, and indeed to keep it from being detrimental, feedback must be given in an open and constructive way from a frame of mind that seeks to provide objective insight. It must be made clear that this is not a forum for airing personal grievances, and anyone who feels that cannot be even handed and objective should not be permitted to give feedback to a co-worker or direct report.

♦ Feedback should tie to the behaviours, skills and qualities of the individual that will support the objectives of the organisation and that person's role within the company.

♦ Feedback must be reported to the employee in an objective manner, coupled with a coaching environment. If this is approached by the manager as a method to prove any personal opinions he may have of the employee it will damage their relationship and derail the benefits of the 360 process.

♦ 360-degree feedback should be introduced within the company in areas where it can support the mission, vision and objectives of the company; in many cases, it will not be beneficial to blanket the organisation with this method.

♦ The evaluation instrument must be customized to the roles and responsibilities of the individual's receiving the evaluation. Rating individuals on the wrong criteria for the jobs they do will undermine the process and damage the person receiving the review. Different areas within the organisation serve to achieve the mission and objectives in different ways and the extra effort it will take to customize the review instrument to those criteria will pay off in big ways and validate the integrity of the 360-review process.

♦ Those who do a poor job of giving feedback need to be told. It certainly doesn't help anyone to allow them to continue participating in a 360 feedback programme if they don't embrace the intent of the process.

360-Degree Feedback in the Wrong Hands. There are a great many advantages of a solid 360-degree feedback process for the individual and the organisation; but 360 feedback used improperly or in the wrong hands (managers who are overcome by the Monkey Syndrome) can do irreparable harm. Further, it can undermine the good relationships between employees who work in teams, as well as the interaction between customer-facing employees and their customers/clients. Used improperly by managers, it often becomes a way to assess and place blame for the inadequacies of the manager. It certainly has the potential to escalate the stress level, fear of failure and finger-pointing on the part of employees. It will damage the working relationships between team members and between managers and employees if 360 feedback is used for anything but positive coaching and professional development.

Another affect of 360-degree feedback programmes in the wrong hands is that employees will be very hesitant in giving honest feedback in a situation that obviously is not constructive and well-balanced. Most people will be very reluctant to give any feedback that they feel has the potential of being used unfairly by a manager or be used for retribution or punishment. If they perceive the possibility of negative consequences for both friend and foe, people will tend to neutralize their positive comments as well as their negative ones. In other unhealthy situations, it is possible for vindictive employees to take the opportunity to give slanted or even false feedback on peers with whom they have disagreements in order to improve their own positions. This, of course, won't happen in Lemon organisations because honesty and respect are core qualities in both managers and employees. I have seen it occur, unfortunately, in unhealthy companies where the Monkey Syndrome dominates. Employees who behave as Children in response to their manager's Parent style continue that form of behaviour as it relates to each other, sometimes in the most destructive ways.

I also have seen problems using 360-degree feedback in departments where most of the work is done in groups. It is challenging, but not impossible, to give team-based feedback, but where the success of the collective is dependent on maintaining the team relationships and the delicate balance between individual achievement and group success it must be undertaken carefully and only by those organisations and their managers who are well-grounded in Lemon attributes. There is no room for Parental attitudes and techniques while using a 360 feedback process. Further, high-performing groups will see no need for such close group scrutiny. If they are truly high-performing, they have found a way to support and compliment each other's skills, abilities, behaviours and beliefs in a way that delivers outstanding results, and they will be resistant to processes that they perceive may shake up the successful balance within the group. Conversely, poor-performing groups will shy away from any review methods that could bring to light the deeper levels of their inability to deliver and their own insecurities about their performance. They will view attempts to insert the broader based assessment of a 360 process as a veiled attempt to place blame on the group and individuals within the group. The lesson here is that while both high-performing and poor-performing groups may be resistant to the introduction of 360-degree feedback, it can prove to be beneficial to both if developed and implemented carefully. The assessment criteria and feedback mechanism must be created in a way that takes into account both the individual's single effort and their group contribution. The most important aspects are to carefully consider of whom the feedback is asked and the ways in which the results are revealed. It is in the hands of the manager to handle the 360-degree feedback delivery in a constructive and positive way for each team member. There is less at steak for poor-performing groups, of course, but even in those circumstances individuals may have the potential to perform at or above expectations and this can be damaged if the process is poorly managed.

The Best of 360-Degree Feedback. As I have said, in the right hands and under the proper circumstances a well-executed, well-integrated 360-degree feedback mechanism is one of the best ways to improve performance. Success lies in the hands of the manager ... their attitudes and actions, their ability to teach and model Lemon behaviours, and their commitment to consistent and open communication throughout the process are instrumental to the organisation's successful use of this performance management tool. So, what's good about it? Here's what:

- ◆ Having more feedback sources promotes a well-rounded and more balanced assessment of any single individual.

- ◆ It minimises the possibility that the most recent interaction between a manager and direct report forms the basis for a performance review.

- ◆ Feedback from clients or customers can enhance the individual's understanding of what it takes to serve their needs in a positive and constructive way, and it can contribute to improving the quality, reliability and timeliness of their service delivery. It can highlight both highly positive and highly negative traits that affect their current and future success.

- ◆ Feedback from multiple sources can serve to reduce gender, race, age and lifestyle discrimination that could occur from single-source review processes.

- ◆ 360-degree feedback provides needed information about organisational development needs on a broader scale than single-source performance review programmes.

- ◆ An individual can gain valuable insight about personal career development needs from broad-spectrum performance feedback.

- ◆ 360-feedback from direct reports to a manager, when it is honest and can be delivered without fear of reprisal, can highlight Monkey Syndrome behaviour and other bad management habits to improve a manager's performance.

Just as any performance management system, if poorly understood, communicated and managed, has the potential to damage the individual and hurt their chances for successful professional development, a well-constructed system that includes objective and open 360 feedback from multiple sources will move them ahead and speed their development. In the hands of enlightened and dedicated managers, a 360-degree feedback process will open up vistas of opportunity for talented employees. As with much of what I have shared in this book, the actions and attitudes of the manager in handling 360 feedback tools are critical to achieving the kind of results that mark high-performing organisations. Managers who are able to focus on the actions of their employees over their personalities will be able to use 360 feedback to the best advantage for their direct reports. They will use the opportunity of having input from multiple sources to coach and train their people, to constructively address weak areas or those that need attention, and they will be able to present the feedback in an objective manner. Nothing less than that will contribute to the individual's and organisation's success. Managers who have strong Lemon characteristics look for ways to position even their most "difficult" people to be successful. They have the ability and desire to be dispassionate and fair in presenting feedback that is critical of the direct report's actions or attitudes. And yes, there are some people who will receive feedback that speaks to personality or attitudinal flaws. The Lemon manager will look at that objectively, discard anything that appears vindictive or unkind for its own sake, and focus on feedback that is usable and will help the direct report to improve their dealings with superiors, peers and clients/customers. This is about so much more than simply relating the comments; it is very much about modelling behaviours and teaching employees to change the way they view their own actions.

The Balanced Scorecard

The Balanced Scorecard is a way of measuring organisational performance by aligning the organisation's business strategy to its measurement and management systems. This process focuses on interpreting the business strategy in terms of specific business objectives and measurements. It translates the strategy into concepts that every employee can understand and embrace, and makes them operational. This process was created to add tangible measures to the traditional financial measurement criteria with which an organisation evaluates their performance by looking at the additional factors of the customer or service recipient perspectives, the business processes in place and the learning and

The Balanced Scorecard adds tangible performance measures to traditional financial measurement criteria.

growth taking place within the organisation. By adding these criteria to their performance measures, an organisation is able to track their progress on a broader scale and monitor their success at building capabilities and talent. Furthermore, it ties the achievement of short-term financial targets with longer-term strategic objectives. In a practical sense, this is about ensuring that everyone is pulling together, and that individual department or team objectives align with the overall, overarching strategic objectives of the organisation. Individual and team or department success has little impact on the success and productivity of the organisation as a whole if it is not consistent with the longer-term business direction.

The Balanced Scorecard looks at what is called a "four-perspective framework" for a business to achieve shareholder (or stakeholder) value through continuous improvement in culture, systems and people. The perspectives are:

◆ Financial

◆ Customer

◆ Internal Process

◆ Learning and Growth

These perspectives are tied to each other in a natural sense. Financial success depends upon retaining current customers/clients and attracting new ones; the ability to deliver products or services that meet and exceed customer/client needs and expectations in a timely and cost-effective manner is crucial to customer satisfaction; and fostering talent and resource development (learning and growth) is a critical success factor in aligning the efforts of an organisation's "human capital" to meet customer/client needs and expectations.

The whole concept of the Balanced Scorecard is not an uncomplicated one, but it is best understood by thinking of the organisation as being in total alignment from a financial, service delivery and resource perspective. The Scorecard itself enables leaders to articulate the "value proposition" the organisation brings to the table and frames it in terms that promote planning and evaluation of various segments against broad scale success criteria.

From the performance management perspective, the Balanced Scorecard process seeks to link the financial, customer and strategic processes identified within the value proposition with a totality of competency development, leadership development and performance evaluation. By focusing on developing their human capital, including identifying both high-achievers and those who are missing the mark, a company can focus the professional development of their people in a direction that will support their business strategy, create value for the enterprise and deliver value to the customer/client.

Lessons Learned

I once worked with a client in the public sector during a Balance Scorecard implementation. The new Chief Executive had inherited a successful team that had just been through a challenging period of change with their former Chief Executive. This change process had brought about a significant, positive business turn around. The new Chief Executive, whilst very content with her overall team, recognised there was stretch left in the operation and that some Directors were still carrying members of their departments whose performance was less than stellar. Indeed, a couple of the Directors themselves were probably being carried by the momentum of the business turn around. Their performance was, in fact, being supported by the knowledge that the turnaround had been a success – when in fact, if analysed in isolation, their own performance was nothing better than average.

All of the performance management basics were in place in this organisation, so to move to the next level they needed to use more advanced processes to create a thoroughly customer-centric environment. The Chief Executive and her senior leaders believed that this would maintain cultural momentum, as well as help put a new focus on financial management strategies and keep the drain on local resources to a minimum. The concept of the Balance Scorecard was not unheard of in a public sector operation, but it was certainly a big change for this organisation and a new concept for employees at all levels to understand. Fundamentally, as this programme was rolled-out, the Lemons flourished and the Monkey sufferers attracted attention and were not tolerated. Those throwing their monkeys in the direction of their manager were now more obvious as the manager began to focus on employee behaviours that promoted the department's alignment with the strategic direction. The managers found they could no longer be seen to tolerate monkey-tossing behaviour in their departments, nor could they possibly perform at a satisfactory level while wrangling monkeys and ignoring the coaching, training and management needs of their people. Productivity rose after implementation of the Balanced Scorecard process, and employee numbers (headcount) fell through organic turnover, leaving the business free of the final pieces of dead wood. People at all levels have a tendency to bail out when the heat is turned up, if they are not willing to get on board with a new operational focus.

Absence Management — Improving Company Performance

What is happening inside organisations that have high absentee costs? Unless you live in a country that has experienced a global phenomenon, like a hurricane or tsunami, high absenteeism is not normal. The BBC reported in its Online Business Reporter that absenteeism had reached over 40 million days annually, and of those 13.4 million were due to stress, anxiety and depression. The absentee cost reported was a staggering £11.5bn. Framed another way in a study by the UK Labour Force Survey, the absentee rate in the UK hovered just above 3% during a recent 18-year period. A CBI survey further reported that employees in the public sector took an average of 10.2 sick days, and employees in the private sector took an average of 7.3 days. Whichever way you analyse it, these statistics point out the dramatic impact on the productivity and potential competitive success of businesses in the UK. And we can't disregard the fact that these are averages. While some companies have more favourable statistics, many companies do far worse.

What has always concerned me about the levels of absenteeism in Britain is not that our population appears to tend toward ill health; rather, it is the fact that much of these "illnesses" are the result of circumstances within the workplace rather than physical ailments that plague our citizens. Over one-third of the sick days reported in the BBC Web site article were not due to physical illness or injury, but rather were mental and emotional in origin. For Lemon organisations, absenteeism is not a big issue because they continuously confront and address the cultural, management and organisational issues that so often lead to high levels of absenteeism. Lemon employees are energetic, engaged and enthusiastic. They don't wake up wishing they could pull the bed linens up over their heads and go back to sleep

Over one-third of sick days in the U.K. were due to mental and emotional issues, not physical illness or injury.

for the rest of the day. They are full of zest and eager to get back to the project or issue they were working on the previous day. Lemon employees deal with emotional issues in the workplace with Adult behaviour: they react with less emotion and more thoughtful consideration than employees operating in a Monkey-plagued environment.

In talking with managers and employees throughout the years, I have found that for so many employees it is not an absence or relaxation of absenteeism policies that have any impact on their attendance. These people simply get to the point where they can't face the day in the environment in which they work and are not sufficiently motivated to expend the extra effort it would take to go to the office. Their problem may centre on issues with a colleague or a manager; or it may be caused by their discomfort with or fear of the work they are doing. These causes go back to the way in which the team and department are being managed. It is quite obvious that the manager in such a situation is not addressing personnel issues and is not focussed on guiding, teaching or coaching these employees. Moreover, it is about motivation — Lemons are more self-motivated and have less absence because they are energised and engaged in the work they are doing ... while in a Monkey infested environment employees are not. It's not just that Lemons are able to withstand more stressful encounters within their workplaces, it's that their workplaces are more Lemon-friendly and there are fewer management misadventures with which they have to cope.

Think back to any of the Lessons Learned that we have covered so far. What is the likely outcome of direct reports who work under a manager living the Monkey Syndrome and dealing with them in Parent mode? Imagine the level of absenteeism that occurs on annual performance review day in these organisations because of the stress level employees feel in anticipation of what is to come during their review. I find stressed out, burned out employees within every team run by a Monkey manager who slips into or just stays continuously in the Parent mode. Employees dread their encounters with these managers. They look for opportunities to just bail out and give themselves an emotional break once in a while. And it usually doesn't really matter whether they are in the midst of a big proposal, project or have a load of work to do ... when these employees can't take the pressure and strain of their manager's or a peer's aggressive and, sometimes, abusive behaviour toward them, they have to bail out. They lack the enthusiasm and motivation that pushes Lemons to stay the course.

Most human beings have a fairly high stress tolerance for the normal kinds of 21st century stressors, such as: standing in line at airports and almost everywhere else, road rage, too much to do and not enough free time to do it in, long journeys, lack of relaxation or sleep, sick children, heavy work loads, and demanding clients/customers. However, no human being is prepared to continuously face the flight or fight adrenalin rush of nasty confrontations with managers and peers in the work place, sexual harassment, screaming and anger-filled bosses, loud and vigorous reprimands in public, or the cold shoulder from managers who are repeatedly critical of your performance but refuse to discuss what you should do about it. These are historic behaviours of past eras of Theory X and "Command and Control" management styles, but while business and industry in general have come to embrace a more humanistic approach to management, there are still managers in organisations all over the world who are stuck in detrimental behaviours that keep employees stressed, anxious, and on edge, and stifle their own personal growth as managers. It is my judgment that most of these situations are based in the organisation's inability to cultivate Lemon managers, which perpetuates managers' inabilities to cultivate Lemon employees.

The absentee "code." The reasons employees give when they call in sick are frequently interpreted as code for what is really wrong with them. Employees typically report colds and flu as the number one cause of missing a day in the workplace, which managers typically agree is the legitimate problem, probably because you can hear the symptoms over the phone. However, it starts to go downhill quickly from there. While employees report their illness to be stomach upsets or food poising, managers interpret this as stress and emotional problems. Employees call in to say they have a migraine or back problems, managers assume it is the Monday morning blues or that they are just bored and want to extend the weekend. And when employees admit to their problems being stress-related, managers, on the other hand, translate that into family illness or childcare/elder care problems.

There are many lifestyle issues that contribute to what some refer to as manipulating the absence policy. There are patterns of behaviour that are created by the inflexibility of some policies to accommodate the issues faced by working parents and is a singular issue that occurs worldwide. While many companies are working toward providing more flexibility to help employees achieve work/life balance, I believe the greatest and most pervasive underlying problem still is a work environment that blocks the employee's ability to perform at their best. Any time an individual is not actually ill, but calls in sick for any reason other than family necessity (sick child/parent/spouse); there is a workplace issue that underlies it. Yes, it can possibly be that the employee is unmotivated and is simply the wrong person in the wrong job. However, I would be willing to bet that the manager either has chosen to ignore the situation or is incapable of handling it, because in allowing the problem to perpetuate itself, he is surely taking on that employee's monkeys and is unable to have any meaningful communication or provide acceptable guidance and training. In a few words, the problem is: Monkey Syndrome, Parent mode, no communication.

Finding the balance: business wants — employee wants. There is a balance to be achieved within the business environment that mitigates these absenteeism problems. It is created when managers are able to recognise and support employees' higher level emotional and professional needs, and maintain productivity and competitive edge at the same time. The formula is simple ... drive employee needs for fulfilment, self-actualisation, and self-determination in an environment that recognises their achievements with both financial and non-financial rewards. Although many companies don't realise it, these are really compatible objectives. Here is a comparison of what each side wants:

Businesses Want	Employees Want
Productive employees	Fulfilling work
Brand-proud employees	Pride in the place they work
Employees who are on the job (low absenteeism)	Respect from managers and peers in a supportive working environment
Engaged employees	Career satisfaction
Promotable employees	Career growth opportunities
Retention of key talent	Recognition of achievements and satisfactory performance
Employees they can trust	Managers and a company they can trust

When the company and employee are on the same page, it is not such a stretch of the imagination that the synergies between them can result in a dynamic, high-performing organisation full of motivated employees who are willing to give the extra discretionary effort at the time it will really make a difference to the company. Such a company does not have a high absenteeism rate, but rather has built-in policy flexibility that allows employees to manage their personal and family life issues while, at the same time, giving focussed, concentrated effort to the work at hand. In addition, employees of this high-performing company:

- Get personal satisfaction out of their own achievements and out of contributing to the success of their team

- Are accountable for the decisions made within the authority of their position

- Are clear about their performance targets and what constitutes meeting and exceeding management's expectations

- Have open communication with managers of this company who value their direct reports, treat them with respect and have no reason to question their word if they have to miss a day of work

- Remain free of the Monkey Syndrome and have the time to teach, coach and develop their direct reports in ways that are personally beneficial and organisationally rewarding

- Work in a company where productivity is high and the company is considered by others within its industry to be a leader

- Are managed by individuals who are adept at fostering a culture of learning, trust and mutual respect.

This company is a success and has built a culture capable of cultivating Lemons at all levels within the organisation. They identify and put the best people in the most important positions. Does this describe your company? Don't you wish it did?

Take a look at one company I had the pleasure of working with that learned its lessons and now profits from them through brand equity, low turnover and absenteeism, and high productivity.

Lessons Learned

At this company, I found the best and the worst of all possible situations, which is unusual because the best rarely survives in the atmosphere of the worst. This company was a huge international consultancy serving the top companies in Britain, Europe and the U.S. The company at that time was about 20 years old and had reached its current size and power both through acquisition and organic growth. The Chief Executive had a totally hands-off style, and integrated the senior managers of the acquisition companies into the management team of the managing company. This, however, was the extent of the integration efforts, because this Chief Executive didn't place any value on the need to blend cultures or create unity within the organisation. Consequently, many of the acquired companies retained the qualities and cultures of their previous incarnations when they became business units of this mega-corporation.

You're probably beginning to guess the "worst" factor in this company ... right: it had no unifying culture or values. Yet, it was highly successful, which seems to be an impossible feat of business legerdemain. After spending a few sessions with the senior managers, I knew the source of the "best" for this company ... it was these senior leaders who had come in with their acquired companies. I often wondered how this Chief Executive got so lucky to have chosen companies for acquisition that had really enlightened leadership, when he was so unenlightened. However, this shouldn't be much of a mystery, after all, because the acquisitions were stable, profitable and productive, and embodied many of the qualities of the best Lemon organisations. This became so apparent as the interview process went on and I was able to become more thoroughly acquainted with each of these leaders.

One person who stood out in particular was Margaret, the head of a division that was born out of her highly successful organisational development consultancy. Margaret had not founded the company, but her Lemon-rich style of management turned her team into a powerhouse within the consultancy, and she later became Senior Managing Director. When her company was acquired she moved quite naturally into the position of Senior Manager for the new business unit within the larger organisation. Margaret's personal success came from her highly developed Lemon attitudes and behaviours. She loved her work and she had energy, focus and total dedication. Part of the secret of her success was the total connection she had with the work she did; and part of her success was the skillful way in which she coached, taught, and uplifted her direct reports.

Equally, Elizabeth was a true manager Lemonista ... she focused on the skills, abilities and needs of her direct reports, and she encouraged them to continuously stretch their boundaries and supported them when they did. Elizabeth set the bar high for her team, but she positioned them for success by playing to their strengths and their core competencies while teaching them and encouraging their development of new ones. She was also very skilled at understanding the motivation of each individual and was able to give them the right amount of encouragement, balanced with training. Elizabeth had a critical personal characteristic that made her a successful manager... she respected her direct reports. She understood their need for fulfilling work, pride in the work they did and in their company, and satisfying career progression. Her people respected her, knew they could learn from her, and were completely dedicated to proving her confidence in them. She never failed to celebrate their achievements and encourage them to continue doing better. She managed her time and her own monkeys, but never took on the monkeys of her direct reports. As I worked with this company, I frequently partnered with Elizabeth to use her management skill to help her colleagues deal with their Monkey issues.

The High Cost of Monkeys

We've touched on what the Monkey Syndrome costs organisations in terms of morale, productivity, achievement of excellence, employee absenteeism and turnover, and achieving a competitive edge. Those costs are very real but somewhat difficult to quantify quickly. A few years ago I was working with a client who wasn't convinced at first that being embroiled in the Monkey

Managers and companies caught in the Monkey Syndrome experience a hit to bottom-line revenues.

Syndrome was all that detrimental to his organisation and to his ability to manage effectively. We talked about the managerial qualities he wanted to develop, and he bought into the idea that his feelings of being overwhelmed and burdened with his employee's tasks was a time waster and did not improve the working relationship he had with some of his direct reports. However, he just did not yet grasp an essential issue: it was actually costing him money to be stuck in Monkey management.

As a way to prove the point and raise his "pain" level (read awareness) to the point where he would believe in the need to take action to reverse the downward spiral into Monkey land, I developed the Monkey Calculator. Here's how it works.

Monkey Calculator

Define the Value of Your Time as a Manager

Q1 - How many hours *per month* do you spend dealing with colleagues that pass their monkeys to you?   # hours

Q2 - How much is an hour of your time worth? (if your not sure calculate an average hourly rate):   X your rate
(£ann.sal./12) ÷ 160 regular monthly work hours

= Monthly Time Value

Next, Define the Value of Your Colleagues' Time

Q3 - How many hours are lost per month? (of your direct reports suffering from Monkey Syndrome either in conversation with you or through general inaction and monkey behaviour)

    Direct report 1: # hours
    Direct report 2: # hours
    Direct report 3: # hours
    Direct report Total:

Q4 - How much is their time worth (per hour)?

Direct report 1: hourly rate (calculated from 1/12 of annual salary) using 160 regular monthly hours worked   (Ann. Sal./12) ÷ 160hrs

Direct report 2: hourly rate   (Ann. Sal./12) ÷ 160hrs

Direct report 3: hourly rate   (Ann. Sal./12) ÷ 160hrs

Direct report Total: Average Monthly Direct report Rate   Total rate ÷ 3

Q5 - Stress and Extra Work

Average monthly cost of your stress, if not considered in your answer to Q1 (lost or squandered time at work due to worry, concern, and hassles with direct reports - based on your hourly rate)

Q6 - How long has this been going on? Number of months:

Formula: (Q1 X Q2) + (Q3 X Q4) + Q5 X Q6 = financial effect of Monkey Syndrome

Now that you've had a look at the formula, let's see how the calculation came out for our manager. He has three direct reports in particular who pile the greatest number of Monkeys on him and cause his serious loss of productive time. He has four clients that have new projects ready to be started with whom he hasn't been able to conduct a start-up meeting in the last two months. This situation repeated itself about three months prior to our meeting and he lost one of the pending contracts due to this delay. The results of this calculation will be a big shock for this manager. Looking at the effects of his Monkey behaviour from a bottom-line perspective will really hit home.

Monkey Calculator

Define the Value of Your Time as a Manager

Q1 - How many hours *per month* do you spend dealing with one direct report who passes their monkeys to you?

37 hours

Q2 - How much is an hour of your time worth? (calculate an average hourly rate if you are salaried): (£40,000/12) ÷ 160

£20.84

= £771.08

Next, Define the Value of Your Colleagues' Time

Q3 - How many hours are lost per month (of your direct reports suffering from Monkey Syndrome either in conversation with you or through general inaction and monkey behaviour)

Direct report 1: # hours	16
Direct report 2: # hours	11
Direct report 3: # hours	10
Direct report Total: Total # hours	37

Q4 - How much is their time worth (per hour)?

Direct report 1: rate (£31,000/12) ÷ 160 =	£16.15
Direct report 2: rate (£27,000/12) ÷ 160 =	£14.06
Direct report 3: rate (£26,000/12) ÷ 160 =	£13.54
Direct report Total: Average Monthly Direct report Rate	£43.75 ÷ 3 = £14.58

Q5 – Stress and Extra Work

Average monthly cost of your stress, if not considered in your answer to Q1 (lost or squandered time at work due to worry, concern, and hassles with direct reports - based on your hourly rate)

28 hrs per month @ £20.84 per hour = £583.52

Q6 - How long has this been going on? Number of months:

18

Total Financial Effect of Monkey Syndrome
Formula: (Q1 X Q2) + (Q3 X Q4) + Q5 X Q6

£34093.08

The one thing that speaks louder than anything else to managers who are responsible for delivering on financial objectives is the impact on the bottom line. This exercise convinced this manager that he would not be able to achieve his departmental financial objectives without changing his management methods. Looking at a whopping £34,093.08 loss in productivity (or put another way, the annual salary of one of his direct reports!) really opened his eyes in a devastatingly dramatic way. Later he realised the degradation of the morale and the capabilities of his team was equally devastating, but it took the eye-opening financial effect of this calculation to make him finally commit to taking the positive steps necessary to affect a change in his own management style.

Personal Achievement and Business Objectives

In Lemon organisations the alignment between business objectives and the professional objectives of the A players forms the strong connection to the company's success: the A players are successful and contribute consistently because they **get it**. The organisation has business objectives that position it for superior performance in its industry; and the A player feels a deep-seated commitment to advance the achievement of her company. There are different kinds of commitment and differences in the way the personal success of a high-achiever is connected to the success of the organisation. The significant factor, whatever the business and wherever the A player sits in the organisation, is the fact that there is something compelling about the **business** of the business — the focus — that connects with the personal and professional values and objectives of the individual. When that connection exists, the individual performs not only as an A player, but more importantly with powerfully discernible intent in ways that promote the best interest of the organisation at the same time they promote the success of the individual.

> The best way to describe this convergence of objectives is to illustrate it with the example of a young bio-technician, whom I'll call Jim, who started as a laboratory assistant in a pharmaceutical company and who is now the head of research and development in a scientific research company. Jim graduated from a prestigious university feeling passionate about science and the field of research, but wanted to find an environment outside of academia in which his work would be put to practical use. He had specific professional objectives and approached finding an employer in much the same way he did his other scientific endeavours: methodically, logically and unemotionally. Initially Jim thought that a pharmaceutical company was not too commercial a venture for his aspirations. He saw himself as something of a Jonas Salk (developer of the polio vaccine), in need of an environment in which he could incubate his ideas, but at the accelerated pace of the 21st century. He hadn't thought much about his personal values or the kind of organisation that would nurture his creativity, his passion and his search for answers. Jim interviewed with many laboratories, pharmaceutical companies and bio-technology development companies and settled on a mid-sized company that was interested in pioneering nano-technology. This wasn't his main field of interest but he appreciated what he perceived as their entrepreneurial spirit and their eagerness to get products to market that would make a difference.
>
> What he found, however, was a company that, in their zeal to lead what they characterised as the nano-technology revolution, was willing to

reward researchers who wanted to cut corners and skip steps. Consequently, Jim's attitude started to take a dive early on because he saw people rewarded for behaviour that he found offensive and border-line unethical. Deciding to try to ignore the "norm" and march to his own drummer, he created a timetable for his own research that allowed him to build in redundant validations and other research verification techniques that he had learned would protect the integrity of the ultimate outcome and avoid the slightest possibility of creating an end product that he wasn't absolutely positive would be safe and effective. His own drum, however, beat at a tempo much below that of this warp-speed driven company, so Jim began to get the reputation as an insecure plodder who needed a lot of oversight. His managers, thinking he wasn't a self-starter or capable of leading a project with enthusiasm, moved him to secondary projects under multiple reporting layers. Jim, in effect, lost his Lemon lustre and became a monkey-thrower. He saw the trend to require more and more approvals before he could go forward and, for the moment he lost his internal drive and gave up, adopting the Monkey Syndrome behaviours of his lower-performing colleagues. He took everything to his manager for approval ... not because he felt everything needed anyone's final endorsement other than his own, but because he had become embroiled in a division within the company that was run by Monkey managers. The zest had left the team, and they were considered plodders, resulting in their being assigned the back-up projects that didn't have the "sex appeal" of the ones the company considered market place stars.

Needless to say neither Jim nor this company were satisfied by this turn of events. They had hoped to have hired a whiz kid who was eager to jump in and send products and solutions to market quickly. Jim had hoped for a company where he would be allowed to stretch scientific boundaries and his own creative brain-power, but assumed he would be allowed to cover what he felt were necessary bases to protect the safety and health of the consumer. This story isn't about whether Jim is right or the company is right: the story is about a complete disconnect between the values and principles of the company and the employee. In order for Jim to be successful and achieve his objectives of developing leading edge technology that will improve the length and quality of lives, he needs a company that isn't counting on, what seems in research terms, instant gratification. And to find such a company he needs to be completely aware of his own professional boundaries and able to articulate the aspects of a working environment in which he can achieve his potential. Conversely, he needs to be able to analyse how the mission of the company he is considering will support his professional needs, and the way in which his research style will promote the achievement objectives of that company so he can ensure that his values match the critical success factors of the company he joins. Speed to market at its most extreme is at very great odds with ensuring that all safety measures that can be employed have been taken, in some industries, especially where lives are at risk. For a Lemon company to harvest Lemon achievers both the business intent and the business process must be synchronous for employee and management. Neither will be able to reach their objectives, because the ultimate objectives — in this case, being first with a solution (company) vs. guaranteeing safety (Jim) — will forever be incongruous. Something has to give because mutually exclusive approaches will always collide. No Lemons here!

Over the years I have heard managers talk about their philosophical disagreements with the company's management direction, and I have observed those people struggle to achieve success in organisations with whom they do not share a vision of what their work is about. It isn't easy to know at the outset which business strategies will resonate and which will end up in conflict with your personal value set. Everything evolves over time, and there are no guarantees that unexpected events won't befall a currently well-matched manager—organisation pairing that will completely change their working relationship. I've also seen many instances of company direction taking an unexpected turn after which a manager finds herself on the philosophically wrong side of the table. What doesn't work at all is for that manager either to continue to do what she has always done within the context of her role or to force herself into patterns of behaviour that are in conflict with her self-image as a professional.

It often feels that these sharp right organisational turns happen overnight. One day you realise that a complete change has taken place while you were conducting business as usual, and you find, for example, that the successful company that valued a teaching—learning environment and cultivated a vision for success by nurturing long-term business relationships has suddenly begun to hire outside "experts" to rapidly increase sales and revenue on a project basis. Few but those at the top will be privy to the reasoning behind this move ... likely it is financial pressure from stockholders or owners coupled with a downturn in business prospects ... but those details are most often left out of both organisational and management communication. The net effect on the "average" employee, especially the Lemons, will be a radical turnaround from their previous operating concepts.

What happens after that is not pretty. People end up resentful, confused by the change without explanation, and frustrated by a radical new management style, to which many will be unable to adjust. To progress over time from a customer-centric organisation, for example, to a "billable hour" focussed organisation (or vice versa) is disturbing and may be a hard adjustment for many people, but given time and the right training/coaching for managers, it can be done successfully. For a management group to expect this shift to occur swiftly enough to produce large financial gains in a short time frame, is very unrealistic because it turns upside down the image employees have of who they are in their business environments. It also creates conflicts between those people whose philosophies connect with the new direction and those who feel they must fight to maintain their prior business perspectives. This level of organisational upheaval and individual conflict is a breeding ground for the Monkey Syndrome: managers determined to make the shift, whether they really embrace the new philosophy or not, dig in and start taking over control of decision-making and action-taking, particularly from those who are having a difficult time making the adjustment.

> **Lemons focus on results over efforts and tasks.**

Results vs. activities. So what is the real motivating connection between a Lemon's personal success and the achievement of the organisation's business objectives? I believe the key is that Lemons focus on results over efforts and tasks. For example, the meeting they have coming up in 10 minutes is one step toward the end result of a project, not the objective of the project. Lemons seek to achieve on a larger scale because they can "see" the company vision in their mind's eye ... senior management of the Lemon company has been able to articulate clearly enough the overarching purpose and the end objective of their business, not just the product or business market. Both are critical to this symbiosis of achievement ... a Lemon company, which has a clearly and frequently articulated vision that is translated into actionable objectives, and a Lemon employee who seeks the ways to achieve their results that will best contribute to their success, to the success of the organisation as a whole, and also to the success of their colleagues. Lemons see the mission beyond the tasks, which is evident in the way Lemon managers describe their roles. You hear Lemon managers describe what they do using phrases like "my team researches and determines the new products that our customers will want in the future" rather than "I manage 100 people in this research and development division." The difference is distinctive and almost palpable – the person focussed on results speaks first about what she seeks to accomplish, while person who is embroiled in managing tasks is focussed on the execution of the tasks. In focusing on results and the commitment it will take from her to achieve those results, a Lemon looks outside herself, using what she has and who she is to accomplish her personal objectives, and at the same time, contribute to the results of her team and the whole organisation.

Values Count. To be successful, an individual must understand what they value in themselves and in their organisation. If the values are inconsistent, there will eventually be a conflict. Further, what the individual values must, in the end, be the guardian of the work they do. It is certainly possible for someone to be successful doing something that goes against his value system for a period of time, but eventually it catches up with him and manifests itself in ways that are personally self-defeating and organisationally destructive. For example, an individual, even a high-performer considered by his company to be a Lemon achiever, may be able to quite successfully manage the finance function of a company for a number of years. However, if his values are centred in people and in making a difference in their lives, no matter how well he manages the numbers, eventually he will become dissatisfied and it will affect his performance and ultimately to his ability to positively contribute to the organisation's business objectives. What happened to create this disconnect was the individual's inability to discern the difference between what he was good at doing and where his values lay. He may even understand and share the big-picture vision of his organisation, but he won't feel fulfilled by his or his company's success in the long run because he will not be able to devote his life to that endeavour and feel he truly is making a contribution that counts. To continue down that path is what turns Lemons back into Monkey managers: they lose the vision and feel ever-increasing conflict between what drives them to achieve on a personal level and the overarching direction and purpose of the company.

Succession Planning for a Clear Future

No company can survive without a well-formulated plan to replace its key players when the time comes for them to move on through retirement or other departure, yet succession planning is often the last thing on the minds of the Board of Directors and Managing Director. Dealing with current marketplace challenges and working out ways to increase productivity always seem so much more compelling and immediate that they take precedence over planning beyond the coming five years or so. Few leaders at the top perceive the potential business threat of losing a key player due to either unplanned or planned circumstances. Further, they fail to take into account the problem of losing top talent through attrition because that person doesn't see a career progression opportunity that presents a compelling future. The risk of this inattention is that the senior talent pool will be left with either outdated skills or a lack of the necessary leadership attributes to keep the company energised and able to sustain the current level of market competitiveness.

One of my most successful clients told me a few years ago that what keeps him up at night most frequently is the idea that his management team will be on an air plane together and the plane will go down. The loss of life was a horrifying concept to him, but equally terrifying was the idea that his company would be left without any leadership. He had spent years building his business into the leading company in his market niche and the thought of all that hard work being lost in an instant was almost more than he could bear. This individual was the owner of a mid-sized, successful company that had an unblemished 30-year reputation for quality and service. That success had been made even sweeter for him in recent years when he had been able to settle his organisation into a routine of open communication and a focus on internal training and coaching. He was exceedingly proud of the high performers that had demonstrated their own excellence in product design development and customer service, and had rewarded them with promotions and commensurate salary increases. He enjoyed their input at management meetings because they brought a fresh perspective and challenged the existing thinking of the management team, most of whom had been in place for several years, with their new ideas. He was, however, grateful that he still had three long-term managers who had been with him since the beginning, because he was aware that the younger stars still had some growing to do. They needed seasoning in the industry to learn to become a bit more circumspect about how far to push their leading edge thinking. And this was the sticking point for him. With no intermediate layers of experienced managers to help provide perspective and buffer the rawness of his newest high-performers, if something happened to his senior team, he was very much afraid of the consequences to his company. And he was right ... without a succession plan his company was very vulnerable. He was lucky to have stars on the horizon who were providing energy and creativity, but he did need the grounding that more experienced managers would bring to the table.

Succession planning is something that takes the vision of those at the very top of the house to embed into the core processes of the business. It can't be a sideline activity left solely to the Human Resources Department, because it is not about simply filling positions. It is about developing the leaders of the future that will move the company forward. Some organisations approach the issue by identifying external candidates to keep as a cadre of "options" for the future. The problem I see with that approach is that when an external candidate is selected and finally is brought into the organisation she will have no clear knowledge of the Managing Director's vision of the future, no appreciation of the ways in which the organisation evolved and grew into the company it has become, nor any idea of what it took to carve out its place within the industry. All this and more will be outside the frame of reference of that newcomer to the management team. It would be far better to identify high-performing internal candidates who understand the culture and what makes the company tick. Grooming these individuals through leadership development programmes and a progression through various areas of responsibility within the company will ensure that they know the business from the inside out. Keeping them focussed on a professional development path will identify the personal qualities and instil in them the professional characteristics necessary to run the business in a way that upholds the culture of the organisation, while at the same time giving them the practical business experience to prepare them to make critical operational decisions. Working by the side of successful leaders will ensure that they take the reins as qualified, capable managers who remain Lemons rather than succumbing to the Monkey Syndrome.

Why do the top managers in top companies avoid or put off dealing with the issue of succession planning? It certainly isn't because they don't realise how critical it is to the future life of the company to nurture a rich talent pool of capable future leaders. And it isn't because they don't understand that, without them, the company will falter. What many experts, including myself, feel is that it seems, to these managers, almost ghoulish to plan for your own demise — and "demise" is the way they picture it in their own minds. Few of these top-level managers would ever face dismissal, which would naturally be rather uncomfortable to plan for, but they will eventually retire, and retirement, for active, focussed, driven leaders, is almost as unthinkable. What I advise these leaders to do is gear up and start thinking like Lemons about this issue.

Focusing them on the rewarding aspects of having a second line of management defence allows these managing directors and senior managers to get out of the mental box they put themselves in over the certainty of their own future departures. Equally important is building a solid programme of leadership development, with the support and participation of the board, which is incorporated into the fabric of management. Success in succession planning is about identifying, teaching, guiding, coaching, and grooming qualified Lemons who have the initiative, the dedication and the enthusiasm to set and achieve personal objectives that are congruent with the organisation's mission. It's so much more than just finding people who are ripe for development and poised for success: it's very much about finding people within the company whose personal values and vision for a successful future are a total match with the values and the vision of the company. That synergy will be self-sustaining and self-fulfilling, and it is absolutely critical to position talented individuals in key positions in the future.

> **Succession planning is about finding people within the company whose personal values and vision are a total match with that of the company.**

I've heard it said that succession planning deals with making sure you select people who will not bask in the praise and attention lavished upon them once they are identified as high performers and then take off when a "better offer" comes around. I believe it is really a merging of philosophies ... that which is embedded in the fabric of the company with the individual's personal belief systems, business management principles and leadership qualities. When a Lemon organisation aligns its leadership development concepts with its strategic business imperatives it is truly engaging in the practice of cultivating Lemons because it is putting the best of itself into the professional development of the future leaders of the company. The way the company does its business becomes the conduit for the field work that trains, coaches and cultivates more Lemon managers who have the vision and are capable of leading the company into the future with the same energy, vision and zest that made it the company it is today.

What can derail the process of cultivating future lemon leaders? A lot of the same things that derail managers in day-to-day operations can create obstacles in the course of leadership development: too little emphasis on teaching and too much concentration on tasks, along with a failure to look at the critical competencies that are being demonstrated by the most outstanding employees. The leaders of the future will show up ... they will come into the organisation looking for ways to contribute and to make a difference. If they are identified and cultivated, they will thrive. A lot depends on whether an organisation is hiring the right people and putting them in the right jobs. Assuming that is taking place effectively, then the rest is up to the managers who watch these people stretch beyond their boundaries, capture the essence of the organisation's purpose and direction, and actively seek opportunities to make a significant contribution to the results of their team. These people are not hard to spot, though a manager in the throes of the Monkey Syndrome may well interpret the actions of these individuals as out of bounds and will attempt to quash their enthusiasm and energy. You see ... a lot has to fall into place to make any organisation truly a Lemon, but the potential is always there.

Here are some of the must-do actions of visionary organisations that want to ensure the guiding principles and overarching business purpose continues with the next generation of leaders:

- Target your talent-weak areas for concerted planning and development: look at the short term vs. long term talent needs, plot who may go out first because of a poor fit or pending retirement, and calculate which areas of bench strength you need to fill first.

- Involve the business units both in assessing their needs and in determining the solutions so the top performers will be able touch as many aspects of management within that unit as possible, and so these individuals will become known and trusted before they have to assume their future roles.

- ◆ Share talent between units to ensure that those who move up to the broader senior management level have a deep knowledge of all operational aspects of the company ... this is the way to ensure that each top performer understands and shares the total vision for the future of the company.

- ◆ Keep reinforcing the company's brand identity, strategic direction and vision for the future throughout the official leadership development programme and within the deeper coaching relationships.

- ◆ Ensure your programme is embedded in the performance management process at all levels in the organisation so that A players are being groomed early and often and that their progression and development is very visible and can be tracked easily.

- ◆ Let the A players know they have been identified ... this shouldn't be a secret. Organisations gain nothing by keeping their future leaders in the dark about their intentions. These star players will continue to develop their talents and capabilities, as well as their own ambitions and desires. If they are unaware they are being considered for future leadership positions, they may feel the doors are closed to them within their current organisation and that, in order to achieve their personal, professional objectives, they will have to seek out another organisation.

Succession planning is a business art form. It takes away from what task-oriented managers feel they must to do survive. But isn't that really the difference between Lemons and Monkeys? It's an inability to focus on what will build the organisation into a healthier competitor and stronger brand because of an excessive focus on task efforts to the detriment of the professional development and performance management of a workforce with the potential to excel under the right leadership.

Lessons Learned

A few years ago I worked with a major manufacturing client, with some specialised and highly technological functions. With a UK work force of about 10,000 people, the majority of the business was concentrated on factory production, administrative services and supply functions. As I got to know this company better, I quickly found that it was a male dominated environment that needed to address their lack of gender balance, especially in senior management roles. Equally, there was a serious need within this company to cultivate Lemons. Both of these concerns centred on the issue of succession planning.

This company focussed their attention on these needs and, through a targeted succession planning programme, as well as other various initiatives, the client significantly improved the outcomes for women in its organisation over a 6-year period.

One measure illustrating the improvement this company was able to make is the dramatic increase in the number of female senior and departmental managers. Six years previously, the client had two female senior managers. Today, six years after the company modified its corporate succession planning programme to incorporate the company's diversity objectives and sought to accelerate the advancement of women and ethnic minorities within the organisation, the business now has 51 female senior managers.

In the earlier part of the 21st Century, I worked in partnership with this business to redesign its established succession planning process to make the development of women an important priority. My work with them began with reviewing and redesigning their succession strategy. Part of the redesign involved engaging a diversity agenda they had established but not embraced within their succession planning approach. To bring the process of diversity and inclusion to life within the company, I worked with senior management to create objectives that would foster and sustain this important aspect of succession planning in this Lemon organisation.

As part of the review the business set a clear objective for itself: within ten years the number of women at all levels of management should be representative of the number of women in the available talent pool. They also made a commitment that every year at least three women would be among the twenty to forty people appointed to senior positions throughout the whole company.

This strategy guaranteed that women, as well as men, are not only identified as high potential managers, but also that they progress in their careers within the organisation. The career progression programme has recently been amended to engage fully with recent discrimination laws around race, disability, gender, lifestyle preference and age, which also supports the associated concepts of diversity and inclusivity.

The new process of identifying 'high potentials' requires each department to submit a list of candidates, which ensures that no department can opt out through neglect or intentional lack of attention. Career development plans are prepared for each high potential individual and their progress through the company is then 'tracked'. If an identified high potential leaves or falls off the list in the future, the individual's manager must explain why this happened, further embedding the attention necessary for each department to fully engage in this programme.

To counter the perception that most women are still in the 'feeder pool', a replacement chart was created to identify key positions along with the names of three people who could fill each one. It includes the following:

- ◆ Row one identifies the immediate successor.

- ◆ Row two shows the person who should succeed the incumbent if the company had three to five years to prepare.

- ◆ Row three shows the most qualified woman at that time, in addition to any women already on line one or two. Women are included even if it means hiring externally.

But this was just the start. Other key elements of the Succession Planning programme include:

1. Career Planning: Individuals receive guidance to set career objectives and develop the strategies through which they will achieve them. Managers responsible for these high potential employees guide them in plotting their career course and staying on track.

2. Informal Mentoring: Senior managers are encouraged to seek out opportunities to mentor women across the whole business, regardless of the function either represents.

3. Business Rationale: Senior managers of this client will actively promote the link between the succession planning initiative and the company's business objectives of pursuing quality, productivity, new markets and profits. Emphasis is placed on the business success that can flow from having a socially, ethnically, racially and gender diverse workforce, and the recognition that their business will benefit from reflecting their customer demographic.

4. Leadership Role: The Chief Executive champions the initiative. Heads of major operational areas are charged with developing plans for meeting diversity objectives. They report quarterly on the progress of these plans to the Chief Executive. The managers and Chief Executive then meet once a year to review and discuss the progress of the initiative, make further plans and set any necessary course corrections that will continue to improve the success of both the succession planning and diversity initiatives.

5. Senior Manager Involvement: Senior managers are required to keep track of and report on the representation of the defined strategy in their areas.

Succession Planning is a business initiative and as such line managers, not the HR Department, must be responsible for its implementation if it is to be successful. Further, it is necessary to build accountability for fulfilling all aspects of the programme and incorporating them into the performance plans of both line and senior managers. It is too easy for programmes of this kind to get lost or neglected in the day-to-day aspects of running a business. To be successful, it must stay front and centre in the minds and job responsibilities of management.

Critical success factors. To be able to maintain a viable and dynamic succession planning programme, there are key steps that should be included in every one; these are:

◆ Clearly define the organisational objectives for this initiative. Setting a time frame and numbers creates impetus for action.

◆ Create a broad definition of succession planning that will include the widest talent pool.

◆ Ensure that not only are the targeted individuals (representing gender and other aspects of diversity) identified, but that once identified they also are among those being groomed for senior positions. It is never too early in an individual's career to begin nurturing Lemon characteristics and behaviours, as well as the critical skills they will need to assume positions in either line or staff management. It is important to get the feeder people on the 'radar' because once they are on the 'radar,' more attention will be paid to their development at higher management levels and it will be harder for them to be lost within the organisation. Companies cannot wait for successors to 'appear' in management positions – failure to plan means to plan for failure!

◆ Implement careful and strategic planning for the career development of these targeted individuals. Simply identifying them is not enough. There is great value and countless potential benefits in encouraging informal mentoring to support the coaching they will receive from their managers.

♦ Ensure there is strong leadership and commitment from senior management — this will make or break the success of Succession Planning. The initial and on-going personal involvement of the Chief Executive or Managing Director is crucial to success.

♦ Integrate succession planning into business and diversity objectives. A clear link between business objectives and the desired results of the succession planning process will assist in gaining commitment from the organisation and staff. To be successful it must be portrayed as a core issue.

♦ Make managers accountable for the success of the initiative. As it is a business initiative, business people should be responsible and accountable for its delivery. Clearly stating the business advantages helps to cement the "rightness" and logic of it in the minds of staff at all levels.

These critical success factors for succession planning will appear, on the surface, to be too time absorbing to be worth it in the eyes of some senior managers. What they must keep in mind is that the future of their company depends on the skill with which they select, groom, train and progress their future leaders through the organisation. If it is done half-way or without a complete focus on the desired outcome, succession planning will fail. It has done so many times before in companies that took it lightly and neglected the steps.

Key Points Summary

♦ Performance management isn't controlling and corrective ... it is teaching and coaching.

- Competency models must be specific and personal, and designed to identify the skill sets, innate abilities, behaviour patterns, traits, values and motives that influence results.

- The manager in Monkey Syndrome will be unable to focus on managing performance over managing tasks.

- Parent Tell — Do techniques stifle the employee's ability to learn from their experiences.

- When the manager controls the performance management process completely without input from the employee, the employee remains in Child role without the ability to take the initiative.

- Managers living in the Monkey Syndrome perpetuate the victimisation of both themselves and their employees because they are consumed with their need to care for Monkeys; this stifles any real assessment opportunity for the manager or growth opportunity for the employee.

- The primary problem with failed Performance Management Programmes is fear of confrontation ... on the part of both employees and managers.

- Managers must follow Performance Management guidelines to give the programme the integrity it needs to be effective.

- Poor communication throughout the year ensures performance discussions will be uncomfortable surprises for both managers and employees.

- The core of management competency is communication.

- Performance reviews must always be conducted by **Adults**.

- Lemon organisations experience less absenteeism because of their concentration on addressing cultural, management and organisational issues.

- Stressed-out, burned-out employees are symptoms of Monkey managers.

- Managers in Lemon organisations are able to recognise and support employees' higher level professional needs.

- Enlightened Lemon organisations give employees the flexibility to manage personal and family life issues while still giving their best at work.

- The high cost of Monkeys can be calculated as a hit to the bottom-line.

- There is unique synchronicity between the personal and professional objectives and values of high-performing employees and the business vision and objectives of Lemon organisations.

- Lemons focus on results over efforts and tasks.

- Lemons can "see" the company vision in their minds' eyes.

- To be fully committed to a company, the business vision must support the individual's own values.

- Succession planning acknowledges a need for the merging of the philosophies that form the fabric of a company and the individual's personal values and belief systems.

Management In The Adult Style

PERFORMANCE MANAGEMENT SUCCESS RELIES ON MATCHING WHAT IS MEANINGFUL TO THE EMPLOYEE WITH WHAT SUPPORTS THE OBJECTIVES OF THE ORGANISATION

Objective Setting and Your Employee's Ownership

For objectives to have any meaning at all for the individual, they must be directly related to each person's role within the organisation, professional development track and the business unit/department/team objectives that align to the mission and business objectives of the company. When all three are in alignment, then they will be actionable, achievable and realistic, as long as they are SMART. It isn't hard to write SMART objectives for those who focus on defining meaningful objectives that will support the direction of the organisation. SMART objectives help create a line of sight for the employee between what the individual seeks to achieve and where the organisation is going.

> **SMART objectives help create a line of sight for the employee between what they seek to achieve and where the organisation is going.**

How to Write SMART Objectives

1. **What is it that you want to achieve?** The answer to this question is key. To create your objectives, first ask yourself what it is that you want to be different after the objective has been achieved.

2. **Use positive language and statements.** Your objective should be written as a positive statement and should focus on what you want to achieve through the objective, such as:

Develop a new sales process or increase sales by a measure of ABC.

<u>Write down what you need to achieve</u>, not what you are going to do in order to achieve it. For example:

➢ Increase sales, not make more sales calls

➢ Develop a method for manufacturing ABC, not research manufacturing methods.

➢ Produce more of model ABC, not upgrade the systems

3. **Make your objective very specific.** This requires that you think realistically and specifically about your role and the objectives of your team, department and organisation. You are there to support all three of them, and your success will be enhanced if you tie your objectives to the direction they are moving. For example:

➢ Redesign XYZ Process

➢ Complete all actions on 1st quarter plan

➢ Find five new customers

➢ Build new factory

➢ Increase sales by 10%

➢ Complete project ABC on time and within budget

4. **Identify a measure.** How will you know when you have achieved it? Is this a measure anyone else can understand? For example:

➢ Redesign XYZ Process

   • Measure: There will be documentation on new process

➢ Complete all actions on 1st quarter plan

   • Measure: The 1st quarter plan will have been 100% completed

> ➢ Find five new customers

- ◆ Measure: The customer database has increased by five

> ➢ Build a new factory

- ◆ Measure: Factory is fully built and ready for moving in

> ➢ Increase sales by 10%

- ◆ Measure: Sales will have increased to 110% of January's levels

> ➢ Complete project ABC on time and within budget

- ◆ Measure: Project ABC will be complete and within budget.

5. **How long will the objective take?** Identify the stages you will need to go through to achieve your objective. Work out how long each is likely to take. By working through this detail you can set realistic timeframes (tip: some people find it hard to conceptualise time – if you do, simply ask for someone to give their opinion on time required)

6. **Decide on the end date** or completion date and include it in the objective (note: sometimes business demands set the end date for you. If this is the case you may need to adjust the measure of what you can achieve by the date after working through what is involved – remember the balance is between stretching and achievable). For example:

> ➢ "By 30th July sales to be increased by £xxx".

> ➢ By 10th September to have produced new documentation on XYZ process

7. **How will you measure your success?** If you **can't measure** your objective you have probably written what you will be *doing* (tasks) in order to achieve the objective. Make sure you write down what you need to *achieve* (the objective or outcome).

8. **Is your objective SMART?** Most managers know what SMART stands for (definitions vary from company to company) but very few can actually write a SMART objective. When writing your objectives, remember that they should meet the basic criteria of the SMART principle:

> - **S**pecific

> - **M**easurable

> - **A**chievable

> - **R**elevant

> - **T**ime-bound

Key Pointers:

1. Always start the objective with "By (x date)....."

2. (x date) should be a specific newspaper type date, e.g.: 15th September 2008. Although stating "By end of March" is acceptable, saying "By end of Q2" is not.

3. Follow "By (x date)..." with a description of **what** will be different or have been achieved by that date. Do not include **how** detail or any milestones at this point.

4. The objective should only be one sentence and have one key outcome measure only — using the "Umbrella Technique" can help if multiple measures are required — therefore avoid creating more than more measure or 2+ outputs in one objective.

5. Use a 1-10 scale on intangible, quality type measures where harder measures are not available.

Phrases To Be Avoided

There are some ineffective words and phrases you should avoid when writing your objectives. If you have any of these words or phrases in an objective, you probably need to rewrite it. These words lead to non-specific and non-SMART objectives that cannot be measured:

- ◆ Liaise with

- ◆ Work with

- ◆ Champion

- ◆ Develop a relationship with

- ◆ Contribute to

- ◆ Raise the profile of

- ◆ Update knowledge

- ◆ Read

Lets explore some of those words and phrases to be avoided in some detail...

<u>Liaise With</u>

None of these phrases specifies how you will go about achieving your objective. Go back and ask yourself: "Why am I doing this?" Keep asking until you get to what it is you need to achieve.

Think about that first one: "liaise with." If you think you will **Liaise with** the sales force, ask yourself:

"Why am I doing this? How are the sales force important to my objective and what will I be able to accomplish by building a rapport with them or working with them more closely. Here's what you might want to say:

"I want to liaise with the sales force so that my team knows what is selling best."

Next, ask yourself:

"Why do you want to know that?" Think about how the knowledge of what is selling best in your company will enable you to meet an objective. The answer might be this:

"The sooner we know what is required, the more easily we can make it on time."

Follow that with:

"How soon should you make it after the order is received?" And then you get a very specific target of:

"Within two days."

Stating the objective, then ...

So following that line of reasoning you are able to develop a meaningful objective, which becomes:

"By (x date) make sure the sales orders are filled within two days of the order being received."

The **measure** is the *time elapsed* between receiving the order and meeting the order.

Liaising with the sales force is *how* you are going to do it, not *what* you need to achieve.

<u>Develop An Effective Relationship</u>

Suppose you want to be able to work more effectively with a person on your team or in another department (John Smith) who is instrumental in your ability to achieve perform your job. So you create a goal to "develop an effective relationship with John Smith." How can you phrase that as a SMART objective? Again, ask yourself why: "Why do I need to develop an effective relationship with John Smith?" Answer:

"So that our departments can start to work together effectively."

Then think it through specifically: "What do you need to achieve together?"

"I need to make sure that we design and implement the right software to meet his needs."

The objective then becomes:

"By September 15th the new software is installed to meet the needs of R&D."

Equally, it can be helpful to put some milestones in for an objective. This gives you some useful measures. Here is a way to phrase some further measures for this objective:

- ◆ "When the specification is agreed with John Smith."

- ◆ "When the problems are identified by (the target timing and what they are)."

- ◆ "How and when the problems are resolved."

So, you can add this specific language to the objective to further develop it in SMART terms:

"By September 15th the new software is installed to meet the needs of R&D," plus

"By March 15th agree on the software specification with John Smith"

"By March 30th identify any problems with the specification"

"By April 30th resolve any problems"

Note: the above example is an illustration of how to use the umbrella technique to break down an objective using smaller chunks or shorter term SMART objectives that achieve the master umbrella SMART objective.

<u>Contribute To</u>

If your objective is to make a meaningful contribution to the SMT meetings, you will want to think about the reason that this would be a meaningful objective and the ways in which it will advance the goals of your team and department. The thought process goes like this:

Q: Why am I doing this?

> *A: "I want to contribute to the SMT meetings so that they know what the situation is in my department."*

Q: Why do they need to know that? Think about what will be meaningful to the SMT about deeper knowledge of the operation of your department.

> *A: "So that the decisions they make on project TQP are effective."*

Q: Why do those decisions need to be effective? Consider what is the impact, positive or negative, on the company of good decisions for the project?

> *A: "So that we don't make silly mistakes and waste money on this project, and so that it can come in on time and to budget."*

Q: Given that greater level of detail, the objective becomes:

> *A: "Deliver project TQP on time and to budget (the objective), ensuring the SMT have the information they need (how it will be achieved) about when the project is to be delivered and what the spend is against the original budget."*

Along the same lines, here is one I see frequently that is both vague and immeasurable: "Contribute more to team meetings." This will fall like a piece of limp pasta in your objective setting without more definition. Think: "Why am I doing this?" Even if your answer is

"Because my manager said I should" you can give it more depth and meaning, but taking it further in this way:

Q: Why did your manager say you should?

A: *"So people know more about my project."*

Q: Why do people need to know about your project?

A: *"So that they are aware of what I am doing and how it links in with their work."*

Q: How will that help them?

A: *"They will be able to be more effective in their own projects and avoid duplication".*

Phrased in a meaningful way, that is SMART, the objective becomes:

"By (x date) ensure other team members have the information they need about project XYZ"

Raise the Profile Of

Again, without stating specific reasons why "raising the profile" of the new PFN technique will benefit you or your company, it is a meaningless objective. Consider these things:

Q: Why do you want to raise the profile of the PFN technique?

A: *"Because it is better than the old technique."*

Q: What do you want to achieve by letting people know about the new technique?

A: *"I want more people to use it in preference to the old technique."*

Q: Why?

A: *"Because it's more efficient and gives more accurate results"*

Given those reasons, the objective becomes:

"By 1st June ensure everyone is using the PFN technique."

Identify the number/percentage of people that should be using the PFN technique by 1st June. Quantify the way to measure the accuracy of your results. Identify the efficiency of the testing process to ensure the credibility of the measurement.

Update Knowledge

A goal to "update knowledge" is woolly and immeasurable without specifics. If your goal even goes so far as to state you want "to update knowledge in the field of MPRS" it still is not well-enough defined to be SMART. Consider these questions.

Why are you doing this?

"So I am at the leading edge."

Why do you want to be at the leading edge?

"So we can improve the methods in manufacturing."

How much improvement are you targeting?

"10% in efficiency and 15% in quality ratings."

The objective becomes 2 SMART objectives so we can avoid writing 2 measures in the same objective:

"By (x date) improve methods in the factory to increase efficiency by 10%"
"By (x date) improve methods in the factory to increase quality by 15%"

Updating your knowledge is part of *how* you are going to do it achieve (task) not the actual output it will bring about or achieve (objective)

Read...

Simply reading five journals each month, for example, while measurable, is not a meaningful goal unless you tie it to a desired outcome — a reason that you will read the journals, or educate yourself in any other way. Tying the action to the purpose gives it body and enables you to make the quantifiable number — the five journals — an objective that furthers your personal goals and the objectives of your team and department. So, ask yourself?

Why are you doing this?

"To keep my knowledge in the field up to date."

Why do you want to keep your knowledge up to date?

"So that I will be using the most effective techniques available to do my research."

How frequently do these techniques get updated?

"On a monthly basis."

Taking all of those factors together, the objective becomes:

"By (x date) have a system in place to produce a report on technique updates for XYZ each month thereafter."

Reading five journals is not the objective in and of itself, it is part of *how* you are going to do identify updated techniques in your field.

How to Write Personal Development Objectives

There are some kinds of objectives which people find particularly difficult to write. This usually involves ways in which people develop their professional and management skills. Here are some real examples and tips on how to write them effectively.

> ➢ Attend a presentation skills course

Identify what you want to learn and frame that as your objective. This makes it more likely that you will learn it effectively. It also makes it easier to measure. Suppose you need to improve your ability to give presentations. You could phrase your objective in this way:

"Learn how to plan a presentation by 31st October."

The objective would be measured by the following:

> ➢ You are able to plan a presentation

> ➢ You have planned presentations during the measurement period

> ➤ You reduce number of slides in presentations to one per minute in order to be more concise and articulate during your presentation

> ➤ You identify the appropriate number of slides per minute that you should be covering, based on your presentation skills training

> ➤ You reduce the number of words on each slide to achieve a clearer and more professional presentation.

"Coach Mary"

Identify the particular objective you would have for coaching Mary. In what way, specifically, will you coach her? Is it to improve her skills? To help her achieve something? To make her more effective?

"By 5th June ensure Mary finishes project ABC within budget and meets the quality standards."

Coaching her is part of *how* you are going to do it. Your objective will also identify other measurable aspects of the management action of coaching Mary, and would include:

> ➤ When Mary's project is due to be completed, because it impacts your coaching timing for her.

> ➤ The total amount that she spends on the project compared with the budget she has for the project.

> ➤ The quality measures that will be applied to the results Mary delivers through her project.

> ➤ Manage my team effectively

This sort of phrasing is virtually useless for any manager without more specific actions and desired outcomes. There is no way to measure an objective phrased in this way, which makes it useless as a gauge against which to determine how well you have performed as a team manager. To make the management of your team a SMART objective, you will need to consider and include these things:

- How will you know if you have managed your team effectively?

- Will it involve them achieving their objectives?

- Will it involve improved standards in a particular area?

- What would happen if you did not manage them effectively?

Look at the management objective you are writing from this perspective:

"By 31st December ensure the members of my team meet their objectives"

Managing the team effectively is part of *how* you will ensure they meet their objectives by the target date of 31st December. You may want to add some bullet points identifying how you will do it, such as:

"Coach members of the team at least once per month"

"Improve feedback skills"

"Hold review meetings every fortnight"

Include details of the objectives achieved by the team members.

Resolving Common Mistakes in Writing Objectives

Over the course of my consulting, I have found it is very helpful to clarify some of the common mistakes made by objective-writers. There are several that I see repeated in organisations of all kinds. Here is a summary of those common mistakes and some easy solutions to make objectives SMART.

1. **Not having recorded all your achievements.** When you come to your review you won't get credit for things you and your manager have forgotten. Make sure you note down your achievements as you go along throughout the year. You may feel you'll always remember this or that project, but as the months go by and you become buried deeper in the next project and the next, it is very easy for those early achievements to get fuzzy in your mind.

2. **Objectives you can't measure.** If you can't measure it, the objective is probably not the right objective. Rewrite it, looking for ways in which each objective will create an outcome that benefits your team, department and organisation.

3. **Writing what you are going to do** rather than what you need to achieve. For example: "Raise profile of PMD process" instead of "Make sure everyone is using PMD process by 1st August."

4. **No clear priorities or everything as a priority.** Go back to your manager and find out what the priorities are.

5. **Key achievements not included.** Make sure that what you spend the bulk of your time on is included in your objectives. Update your objectives when there are changes.

6. **Recently arising objectives not included.** Update your objectives as new tasks arise.

7. **Irrelevant objectives included**.   Review your objectives regularly (at least once a month). Delete objectives that have become obsolete (in agreement with your manager).

How Many Objectives Should You Have?

Most people will have from four to six main objectives. They can be split into sub-objectives if that is useful. The appropriate number also relates to your position within the company, whether you are charged with leading projects or people, or whether you are a specialist concentrating on one particular project for the year. That project may have sub-objectives, but you would probably frame your primary achievement targets as one or two objectives.

The broader and more varied your job responsibilities, the more objectives you are likely to have, although you will want to stay focussed and not spread the areas in which your performance will be judged too thin. I have seen people come up with fifteen objectives, thinking that they need to put everything on the line all at the same time. While you may have an extremely broad job with fifteen different aspects to it, you should concentrate on broader performance measurement for projects or aspects of your job that bring the highest value to your team, department and company and that are most likely to affect your professional development most significantly. *If you have large numbers of different projects it's alright to have a separate objective for each one.* In fact, it's much better to do this if they all have different deadlines, targets and measures. However, take care not to go over board racking up multiple sub-objectives for each project.

The Acid Test

Imagine it's three weeks before your review. Your manager has been run over by a bus. A new manager from a completely different department takes over. She doesn't know you very well and has no knowledge of the quality or effectiveness of your work. Can you prove to her that you have achieved all your objectives? You will definitely want to be able to do so, or your performance review will be superficial, non-specific, and possibly unduly influenced by the new manager's impressions of your abilities and performance standards based on first impressions and, potentially, here say evidence from outsiders. If a new manager has a negative first impression of you or your work, she may or may not be able to be totally objective. At best, if you are unable to produce convincing documentation about your achievements against objectives for the year (and if you are lucky enough to have a new manager who is a Lemon) you might receive a neutral review, if she recognises that she has not had sufficient opportunity to get to know you and the level at which you perform. If she has Monkey Syndrome tendencies, you might fall victim to snap judgements and any negative impressions, real or imagined, that she has formed about you. You can protect yourself at least against her lack of knowledge about you have accomplished, if you have kept good records of your own performance against your objectives.

There are a number of steps that any individual preparing for a performance review could and should take to make sure that the appraisal considers all the important facts.

Here are things to do during the year to ensure you can document your accomplishments and your performance accurately and thoroughly.

1. **Review your objectives frequently**. Do this at least once a month.

2. **If you think you will have trouble remembering to review your objectives** put a reminder in your diary or organiser or print out a summary.

3. **When the situation changes, update your objectives**. Make sure each objective is still current and relevant.

4. **Delete irrelevant objectives**. Do this when you are updating and reviewing.

5. **Make sure you have a plan for how you are going to achieve each objective**. When you update and check your objectives, check that your plans are still going to work.

6. **Monitor your progress on each objective**. Note down your achievements as you go along. You will have forgotten what you did when it is reviewed 12 month's later.

7. **Check the current situation and how your plan fits in with it**. Does it still work? Update your plan accordingly.

8. **Add new objectives to your plan as they appear**. Make sure you have clear measures for each of them.

No individual should have to fact the "acid test" and be unable to document their accomplishments or ways in which their objectives changed during the year. Change is the watchword in business these days, and no one can count on both their objectives and their reporting relationships remaining static. While it is less likely that a manager will be hit by a bus, it is very likely that a manager — direct report relationship can be changed in mid-year. It is even more likely that circumstances within an organisation, department and/or team will require a complete shift of focus for any given individual, making all or some of his previously outlined objectives moot. To be unable to document the reasons for the adjustment to new projects and objectives is horribly unfair to the individual being reviewed and says some very negative things about an organisation that would condone judging an individual's performance against outdated objectives. I have seen it happen, however. In some cases, in an effort to be fair and in the absence of documentation about the change in direction and new objectives, a new manager may simply give a neutral appraisal ... neither overly positive nor overly negative. That does almost as much a disservice to the individual as a negative appraisal ... almost. What it does is basically remove that entire year of effort from the books. It can also have a negative effect on pay increases and promotion opportunities.

Coaching Skills — Adult to Adult, Not Parent to Child

Coaching in business is a management strategy similar to that used in sports. As you know, in sports, coaching is about working with an athlete to help her achieve her potential and unlock the possibilities of her greatest achievements. Coaching in business, while in a different context and using somewhat different techniques, is an interestingly similar effort. The end result is, within its own context, almost identical in both business and sports... to help the coachee become completely self-aware, self-confident and capable of delivering successful results independently and with enthusiasm.

The very nature of the coaching process demands that the coach operate in the Adult mode. It is not possible to coach someone if you are giving orders and instructing her in exactly what to do and how to do it. Coaching requires more finesse, a lighter touch and a higher degree of belief in the individual's ability to be successful than that which is possessed by the Parent-style manager. It takes a Lemon to be a really good coach. First of all, it is about belief.

A successful coach holds a belief that the individual has the potential and ability to be successful, and the desire to unleash that success.

A successful coach holds a belief that the individual has the potential and ability to be successful and has the desire to help the individual tap into that potential and unleash the success within herself. This is an Adult concept and a very different approach from a Parental attitude applied in the work place that results in the primary effort being to identify the individual's shortcomings and instruct them on how to stop doing the wrong thing. Given that perspective, everyone will fail at some point, even Lemon employees who largely perform at a high level, because no one is perfect and people make mistakes. Looked at through the lens of achievement, a mistake is just a missed opportunity to achieve at or above a person's potential. That is the viewpoint of Lemon managers operating in the Adult mode, and they take the opportunity the mistake affords to help the individual review what happened and expand their thinking to the next level so that the next time around they won't miss the opportunity to exceed expectations and achieve at a higher level.

The critical Parental Monkey manager, on the other hand, looks at any mistake as proof that the individual needs more direction and instruction. Worse yet, as we have seen in earlier chapters, the manager in the throes of the Monkey Syndrome virtually removes any opportunity for the individual to become successful by taking on the care and feeding of her monkeys. Not only is this Monkey-manager doing the obvious to his own productivity, he is also preventing his direct report from taking responsibility and learning from what should be her own experiences. She is unable to build any self-belief or awareness of what it takes for her to be successful because she is giving over her responsibilities and waiting on instructions from her manager.

In Parental mode, the Monkey manager will miss the point of coaching and plough right ahead toward judgment and instruction. Observe the tactics of this Monkey manager in the interaction below:

> Gerard, the manager, has been told he has to perform as coach to his direct reports, in addition to managing their performance. He doesn't really understand this, but determines the best thing for him to do is to do what he always has done, only more of it. That means he will scrutinise the performance of his direct reports on a more frequent basis, and let them know what they need to do to improve their decision-making. Typically, he ends these sessions by taking over the aspect of the project on which he is attempting to "coach" them, justifying those actions by the short deadline, the seriousness of the situation or the importance of the outcome. Unfortunately, he frequently moves on the issues and the performance much too quickly, even before they have had a chance to complete the steps they are taking. Here's a typical conversation:
>
> Gerard ... "I was reading your report on the XYZ project and I see you have missed two important components. Why have you not contacted Marketing about them yet?"

Direct report Thomas ... "Well, I thought I should complete phase one before I move on to that. I was planning to call Marketing next week."

Gerard ... "I told you last week you needed to set up a meeting with Marketing. Why haven't you done as I told you?"

Thomas ... "I was planning on it, but I didn't have time. You see, these three other steps seemed more important to complete right now and I thought it would wait until next week."

Gerard ... "Well, you thought wrong. And you are moving too slowly. Why can't you get this work done? It's not that complicated. You should be doing steps 4, 5, and 6 simultaneously. I really don't know why I put you on this project. I'll take over from here. You just go back to your regular work."

Thomas ... "But ...." and he never gets to finish as Gerard has walked out of the office. He was prepared to explain that there were new facts that came to light in step 3 and that he had consulted a colleague in Engineering who advised him to take a remedial action before moving on. However, Gerard was in no mood to listen to anything Thomas had to say. He had already made up his mind that he would have to step in, and that Thomas was incapable of performing at the level at which he was expected. Thomas is left with the same feeling because his initiative at contacting Engineering and taking appropriate action based on what he found out has met with disapproval and the consequent removal of the project from his responsibility. Not only has Gerard not behaved as a Coach, he has also behaved in the very worst possible Parent mode, causing Thomas to begin to doubt himself and to feel that he can do nothing right in the eyes of his manager. Unfortunately, Thomas is probably right, but not because he isn't capable of achieving his objectives successfully — because he has a bad Coach. Gerard has taken the quickest and, for him, easiest way out. He has cut Thomas off at the knees and taken the Monkeys.

Achieving one's potential and performing at the highest levels requires a belief in the possibilities, self-confidence, commitment, and awareness of and belief in ones abilities. These are the qualities of a Lemon, and they carry a person through temporary failure, mishaps, and obstacles. Lemons can rise above it, even in Monkey driven environments, but they can really thrive in Lemon organisations because they get the support they need to reinforce the qualities of success.

On one level, coaching is about helping the individual build awareness of the opportunities available to her and build awareness of the choices she can make in any given situation that will lead to a successful outcome. When coaching is optimally provided, it leads to successful outcomes that the coachee can look at and realise she achieved through her own efforts, decisions and actions ... that she can take full responsibility for. Those successes build on themselves and lead to further success, in part because it reinforces the individual's confidence in their abilities, in their decision-making, and in themselves. As they say: "Nothing succeeds like success," and the foremost accomplishment the coach should work toward is to help the coachee believe in her ability to do "it" ... whatever it is ... which begins with believing in herself and looking at her strengths and weaknesses honestly and dispassionately. When she can be equally objective about actions she takes that do and do not lead to the results she is striving for, she will be able to learn from her own decisions.

> **Achieving one's potential and performing at the highest levels requires a belief in the possibilities, self-confidence, commitment and awareness.**

Taking on the role of coach for a direct report can be a rather daunting prospect for some managers. Coaching isn't natural for many managers and it requires them to take a different approach than they might otherwise use ... they must suspend their hold on their level of authority over the direct reports pay, promotion and continued employment. In the coaching relationship it is about empathy, understanding and impartiality. The successful coach will above all work to create a partnership with the individual he is coaching that is built on trust and mutual respect. That will enable the coachee to be confident that the coach is working to help her set herself up for success, but will be honest and realistic about the path and the steps she needs to tack to realise her potential.

If Gerard had been a better manager and had been capable of actually coaching Thomas rather than only assessing and dictating, Thomas would have been able to get a response from Gerard that was conducive to learning from the decisions he made. Here's how the conversation could have gone.

> Gerard ... "I read your most recent report and was impressed with the level of detail that you included in it. I wonder if you could give me a bit more information about the marketing issues we discussed last week."

> Thomas ... "I know they are critical, but as I was completing step 3 a question came up about RB27 and I consulted Jon in Engineering. He told me about the research they are doing and the impact it will have on the future of the project. I feel that before we finalize anything with Marketing, I need to be able to incorporate the information I received from Jon into steps 4, 5, and 6. I thought it would be fine to wait until next week to get with Marketing."

> Gerard ... "I see. What you tell me does make sense. Have you formalised a schedule adjustment?"

> Thomas ... "No. I didn't know that would be important."

> Gerard ... "Do you know whether it would be holding anything up in Operations if our schedule is adjusted?"

> Thomas ... "Actually, no."

> Gerard ... "That would be good to know. I'll leave it to you to work through it and if there is any problem, let me know. Otherwise, keep going as you are. Also, have you alerted Marketing to the change in the schedule?"

> Thomas ... "Well, no. I haven't had time."

Gerard ... "I know you are really pushing to meet this timetable, but keeping Marketing on our side in this project will be instrumental in getting the rollout we need."

Thomas ... "Yes, I do realise that. I should have sent a note to them. I'll get on that right away."

Gerard ... "Great. As you take on more of these projects, you'll be able to catch the bigger picture issues easily. I'm proud of the work you are doing."

Not only did Gerard give Thomas a chance to tell him everything he needed to know, his interaction with Thomas was positive, non-judgmental and supportive. He gave Thomas an opportunity to work out some of the nuances of running a major project for himself. Because Gerard asked questions instead of assessing and accusing Thomas of letting the team down, Thomas came to some conclusions on his own, took responsibility for addressing a couple of deficiencies and ended the discussion with an overall feeling of success punctuated with next steps that would keep the project going in the right direction. The manager as coach has both the fate of the direct report in his hands and the future of the coachee's ability to perceive changes in direction and attitude that will lead them to more successful outcomes.

In the second scenario, Thomas learned a key lesson in project management: in the midst of <u>doing</u> it is essential to maintain a broader view of the project in order to manage expectations and keep surprises for others involved in the project to a minimum. No one likes surprises in business because they are rarely the warm and fuzzy kind; certainly no one likes to find out things at the last minute that will cause time schedules to go awry and mean more work for them that is caused by the lack of action by another party. In being lax about communication, Thomas runs the risk of Marketing getting in a snit about not receiving notice that the time frame would need to shift. In turn, this could knock this project off the radar and lose them needed Marketing support. This was really a very big deal, but rather than accuse, rant and rip the project out of the hands of the hapless Thomas, Gerard allowed him to come to the awareness of the critical nature of the situation without recriminations or drama, and rectify the situation before it became the project-killer it could have been.

Feedback Skills — Controlling Your Parent Tendencies

Giving feedback is a critical skill for a Lemon manager. You can make or break the performance of your direct reports by the way in which you give feedback. You can create a bond with them that will ensure their cooperation and build loyalty; at the same time, if mishandled in the Monkey Syndrome Parental Tell-Do style, your feedback methods can set up a perpetually distrustful and adversarial relationship with your direct report, which you might never be able to turn around. If your feedback is intended to be positive, it must have a ring of truth. If your direct report suspects your praise is in any way self-serving — e.g. designed to get them to "do" something they probably will not want to do or in an underhanded way praise your own management style — or insincere or too effusive, you will lose him immediately. He will feel you have some hidden agenda and that your motives for giving that sort of feedback are dishonest or underhanded. Conversely, if your approach is open, disingenuous, and authentic, your direct report will believe that his is truly meeting or exceeding your expectations, feel energized by the praise and desire to keep doing what results in such feedback. You will be building Lemon characteristics and positioning the direct report for future success.

> **Feedback is information about your actions and their consequences that helps you to learn.**

Suppose your feedback needs to address skill deficiencies or behaviours that are counter productive to the team/department. Once again, you feedback approach can make or break this encounter with your direct report. If you use a Parental Tell-Do style ... meaning that your tone is accusatory or aggressive and you approach the direct report as a parent listing their child's transgressions ... you will lose the respect of your direct report and position your feedback as retribution rather than anything that can be acted upon to improve performance. Addressing skill deficiencies is much easier than behaviours, but both require a sensitivity that escapes many managers. Remembering that the direct report is deserving of your respect, regardless of their performance inadequacies is the key to achieving a Lemon approach. Lemons beget Lemons, and if you want to cultivate a team of Lemon direct reports you must treat them with respect and focus on coaching and teaching to achieve desired behaviours and actions over controlling and disciplining them.

Receiving feedback is also a challenge for many, and managers often are in a position to receive feedback from their direct reports; and in order to be able to teach a direct report how to receive feedback in a constructive way, every manager must possess the skill to **get** feedback with an open-minded and optimistic attitude.

How to Give and Get Feedback

Here are some tips on how to give, as well as get, Lemon-filled feedback.

1. *What is feedback?*

> Feedback is information about your actions and their consequences that helps you to learn. Without feedback there is no learning. If you are a manager it is your responsibility to ensure that an individual gets the feedback they need in a form they can understand.

> There is no such thing as 'positive' or 'negative' feedback. True feedback is factual information and is based on what an individual did or said, not on someone's opinion.

> Feedback is not about who a person is, or their 'identity'. "He is an idiot." "She is the ideal candidate." "She just isn't at the right

level yet." "He's great." These are opinions and should never be part of your feedback language.

2. Why give feedback?

Without feedback there is no learning. Feedback enables a person to improve their performance or to sustain already effective performance.

3. How does it help?

Understanding the impact of you actions helps you to make better decisions on what to do next time.

4. What are the objectives?

To make sure a person knows what they need to do in the future to improve performance or maintain excellent performance.

5. What forms can feedback take and which is most effective?

➢ Feedback can be something that comes in through any of your five senses. Normally it is spoken, so you hear it. A chef would often be seeking feedback from taste or smell.

➢ Hearing verbal feedback is often the most ineffective route for many people, especially those who are primarily auditory learners.

➢ Experiencing something — through feelings, by doing it or by seeing it — can be a much more effective route for many. Adults learn especially by "doing," so experiential learning is very effective for most adults.

Giving Feedback to Others: Comparison of Different Methods

There are advantages and disadvantages of different feedback methods. Some people fine the best method is to ask questions so the individual to which you are giving the feedback can have a greater part in the feedback process. However the most prevalently used feedback method is the "Tell" method, where the feedback is given in the form of statements made to the receiver. Both can be effective, though the "Tell" method can come across as judgemental and rigid if the manager isn't careful about how the feedback is handled.

Feedback Through Questions – How Do You Do It?

You ask questions. While you are asking questions:

- The individual takes responsibility for the feedback

- The individual takes part in the feedback process

- The individual works it out for himself ... their own answers to the questions create the feedback you are seeking to impart to them

- The individual has to think about what he has done, how he has done it and how that has worked for him

- The individual is convinced by what he says ... after all, it his own words he is contemplating

- The individual is more likely to understand the feedback correctly ... the individual understands his own comments, and has appropriately responded to the questions you have posed

All feedback should focus on facts not opinions, on the actions of the person, not the person.

- Performance substantially improves as a result of the realisations that come to the individual during the question and answer process.

You, as the manager, have a lot of responsibility here: you have to come up with questions. You have to think. You have to make sure that the questions you pose will illicit the kind of thinking that will move your direct report to both the understanding of the messages you are sending and the action you are looking for him to being taking.

- However, the answers you receive from your direct report may be different than the ones you were expecting so you need to be prepared to think on your feet.

- You also have to be patient: generally it takes longer work through a Q&A feedback process than telling the individual your opinions of his performance.

- You give effective feedback to the answers you receive from your direct report.

- If all goes well, performance is improved.

However, a troubled, obstinate or antagonistic individual may not listen to your questions and may disagree with what you say as well as the way your questions are phrased. Also, the individual may not understand the feedback completely when given in this manner. You will have to be very thoughtful about how you compose your questions.

What happens if you give ineffective feedback? Not surprisingly, it is easy to do. If this happens, the individual's effectiveness can be reduced by over 25%.

So, consider your options: feedback through questions; feedback through telling; giving ineffective feedback. Think about these feedback alternatives:

If you phrase your feedback as questions, they may look like this:

- Do you remember the meeting with Tim yesterday?

- Do you remember what you said to Tim?

- What did he say?

- What happened?

- What was his body language?

- How do you think he felt about that?

- What was it you wanted to achieve?

- How do you think you could achieve it next time?

- How many did you sell in October?

- What were the overall sales?

- What will you do next time?

- How could what you have learned be used to help the rest of the team?

Compare this to the "Tell" approach alternative, and consider it's effectiveness in achieving the desired result against the questioning alternative.

- Yesterday in the meeting with Tim you said 'This piece of research is rubbish.'

- Tim looked very upset by that comment. Next time please discuss your thoughts on his work with me before making any comments.

- You increased sales by £57,000 over last year. Please let everyone know what you did to achieve that so they can do the same.

- Your interpersonal skills are poor.

- You are aggressive.

- Sales look good – well done.

What if you have to give corrective feedback? There are alternatives to how you approach this presented by the two feedback techniques. Here's an example. Suppose you need to deal with a situation where the project a direct report handled was over budget and had other problems. Think about questioning vs. direct feedback.

Questioning:

- What was the result?

- What was your original plan?

- How did you decide on that course of action?

- How did the team members respond to the problems?

- Did you ask them for their feedback?

- What did they say to you?

- What skills do you think you need to improve on?

In contrast, here is a summary of the direct feedback method:

- The software was over budget by £40,000 and still doesn't meet the requirements.

- Next time you need to check the prices and the requirements more carefully.

- The project was an unmitigated disaster.

- You are useless.

Look at another example of a situation where a serious error was made in a customer's order and the alternative ways the manager could approach it.

- What did the customer order? What did they receive?

- When did they receive the meals they had asked for? How did that happen?

By comparison, the direct feedback method could proceed, in Monkey mode, in this manner:

- The customers didn't receive the meals they ordered. They had to wait nearly an hour for their meal and then only three of them got any food. The vegetables didn't arrive till they had eaten the meat. The other two people at the table didn't get their first course till their friends had finished.

- This is unacceptable.

- Next time get the order right and make sure it gets to the customer on time.

- You are a waste of space.

- You are not cut out to be a waiter.

Granted, this last is a very extreme comparison ... not every manager would be as tactless as this one example suggests. However, I have seen many people approach giving direct feedback in just such a tactless fashion, with highly unsatisfactory results.

So, how can you make the whole feedback process more effective, more human, more authentic and more productive so you achieve the outcome you desire and need ... a change in behaviour or improvement in performance? Here's how:

Do your homework before you start so you have the facts at your fingertips. Ask questions, even when you are giving direct feedback. This means that when the individual responds, they are experiencing the answers rather than just listening to your interpretation of their actions/behaviours/performance. It makes the feedback much more effective and much more meaningful to the direct report because it frames it from their perspective rather than just from yours.

In addition to the method, here are more tips for making your feedback more effective and ensuring it accomplishes your objectives.

1. Make sure the individual knows and understands the following:

   ➢ What they did

   ➢ What the impact of their actions was

   ➢ What they need to do next time.

   ➢ Start with what happened.

2. Ask questions that help the person to review the facts:

   ➢ "What happened?"

   ➢ "What did you do?"

   ➢ "What did you say?"

3. Clarify the facts if there's a difference between what they say and your understanding of what happened. Ask some more questions. Remember, your understanding of the situation could be mistaken. Find out all sides before you meet with your direct report and remember that if you have not talked with her yet, you may not have all the facts. Definitely avoid making snap judgements based on what one person has told you. There are always two sides to every situation. You won't build trust and loyalty with a direct report if you believe the first story you hear and act upon it without listening to her version and considering the alternatives. For example, you may be dealing with a difference of opinion between how a project or encounter went from the customer's perspective and from the employee's perspective:

"You are saying things didn't go very well. I have a letter here from the customer thanking us for our efforts. Can you explain what happened?"

Or, it could go like this:

"I thought we'd received a complaint from that customer. You say she is completely satisfied. Can you tell me what happened?"

Or, even like this:

"When I asked Bill about it, he said you were shouting. How could it have come across like that to him?"

4. Show genuine interest. This is not an interrogation; or it certainly shouldn't be conducted as an interrogation. Do not gasp with disbelief or accuse the person of lying if what they say seems to contradict what you think. Just ask more questions.

5. Help the individual to consider the consequences of what they did:

    ➢ "What was the result?"

    ➢ "What was the impact?"

    ➢ "How did John feel about that?"

    ➢ "How do you think that looked to Hilary?"

6. Thank the person or give your feelings if appropriate. This is the time to say things like:

    ➢ "I'm delighted"

    ➢ "You've done a great job"

    ➢ "This has saved our bacon"

Or

    ➢ "I'm sure you'll do a lot better next time"

TURNING MONKEYS INTO LEMONS

> ➢ "I'm very sad this has happened"

> ➢ "I know you'll do your best next time"

7. Check if it will really help to tell the other person what you are feeling. Often, once you've been through the feedback structure (especially where things have gone badly wrong) the other person will be only too clear about how you feel. In this case, there's no need to rub it in.

8. Do not say that you are disappointed or angry you are unless it's clear the individual doesn't realise how you feel and it's really important that they know. Again, you can ask instead of telling them. It's usually much more effective:

> ➢ How do you think I feel about this?

> ➢ How do you think I felt when I saw what had happened/got the results?

> ➢ What do you think I thought when I found out?

9. Ask questions about what the individual will do next time or in the future:

> ➢ "What have you learned?"

> ➢ "What will you do next time?"

> ➢ "Where else could this help?"

10. Make sure you get an answer for each stage before going on to the next one.

11. Tell your direct report how you feel when you are very pleased with what she has done. Even if she seems to know, it's an opportunity to spread some good feelings. Take it. It's always worthwhile. When someone has done a great job think about the popular saying: 'Doing

a good job here is like peeing in your pants when you are wearing black: Nobody notices but you get a warm feeling.

12. Make sure you give feedback when things go well, especially if your direct report exceeds your expectations. It can improve performance far more than complaining when things go wrong. This kind of feedback can improve a person's performance by nearly 40%. It is your most powerful performance improvement tool so make sure you use it!

13. Question the individual to find out what she did that made the difference. Many people will be unaware of what it was. To make sure they do it again, you need to help her find out. Use questions like:

   ➢ "What did you do that was instrumental in achieving this (objective)?"

   ➢ "What did you do differently this time?"

   ➢ "What else do you think you did that could have impacted on this objective/result?"

14. When things have gone badly and you are sure of the facts and the outcomes, use exactly the same steps as before (1 - 13). Equally important is to make sure the individual knows and understands:

   ➢ What they did

   ➢ What the impact of their actions was

   ➢ What they need to do next time

15. Then, if it's appropriate, ask what the plan is to retrieve the situation. Do not focus on what your direct report has done wrong or the mistakes she has made, as this drastically reduces performance and can cause ill feelings and poor motivation.

16. Focus on what needs to be achieved and how it can be done.

17. Concentrate on what you need the individual to do next time and help them to find ways of doing it that will work for them. Don't emphasise personality flaws and faults, as this will not give you the improvements you need.

18. Focus on what the individual has done well and the skills she has. Help her to identify how she can use those skills to improve in other areas.

19. Help her to identify which skills need to be improved or learned.

20. Make sure she is clear about what he needs to do next time and how to do it.

Feedback Through Telling

First and most importantly when you give feedback through "telling" is to make doubly sure you have the facts straight. Don't assume anything, including that accounts of a situation you may have heard from a third party are accurate. Whether that third party is another direct report to yours, a peer to you or a client/customer, it is always possible for human beings to intentionally or unintentionally get the story wrong or to simply skew it with their own perspectives. If you are dealing with something about which you do not have first hand experience, always check out all the angles of the story and embrace the possibilities.

The next step is to refrain from making this personal: always talk about what the person said or did, not who a person is. Here is phrasing to avoid:

- ◆ "You are an idiot."

- ◆ "You are lazy."

- ◆ "You were really helpful."

- "You went to help the new recruit without being asked."

- "You cancelled your holiday to get the document finished."

- "You left the document unfinished."

Instead of focusing on what "you" did, meaning your direct report, use this structure in framing your feedback:

- Facts – what happened/what the individual did

- Impact

- Praise/your feelings if appropriate

- Focus on what you would like them to do next time, for example:

  ➢ "You made some changes to the production equipment."

  ➢ "This has increased the overall output by 5% this month."

  ➢ "I'm delighted. Well done."

  ➢ "Please have a look at the equipment in C Block and do what you can to make improvements there."

  ➢ "Mrs Hawkins said you spoke rudely to her when she complained about the colour. She was very offended and has cancelled her order."

  ➢ "Please speak politely to all our customers at all times."

  ➢ "During the interview process you gave two examples of emergency situations where you had not taken control of the

Non-specific praise and negative instructions can have the same effect ... reduce a person's performance ... because it doesn't provide any positive or concrete information on which to act.

situation for at least half an hour." We are looking for someone who has taken control within the first five minutes. This means you have not been successful in your application this time. If you want a job in this field you will need to develop the skills to take control quickly."

> "During the interview process you gave an example of an emergency where you had taken control within a few minutes of the patient arriving. This is one of the key skills we are looking for in applicants. I am pleased to tell you that you are now being put forward for the final round of interviews."

> "We ordered the wine late in the afternoon a day before the dinner and still received it by 4pm the next day with a wine list ready for our guests. This saved us a lot of time and impressed our guests. We are very grateful and will certainly use this 'next day' service again."

> "We ordered one meal and were served a different one that took over an hour to arrive. We did not like the food and were very tired by the time it arrived. Please make sure we get what we order next time and within twenty minutes."

Emphasise the individual's strengths. Research shows that this can drastically improve performance. For example:

◆ "You have developed a great skill in xxxxx."

◆ "It has helped in..." – give specific examples or actual financial benefit.

◆ Give praise; e.g.: "I am very pleased that you did this."

◆ Explain why: "because it meant that..." Always be specific with your praise.

In this way you get the biggest benefit from the praise and it's very motivating for the individual.

Never give general non-specific praise like

"You are great" or "You are amazing."

Astonishingly this can actually reduce a person's performance! This is because the individual does not known what they need to do next time in order to do a good job. This feedback is, above all, tremendously vague ... it gives them no idea what they did to be considered "great" or "amazing." This is how you chat with a pal or family member, not how you give feedback to a direct report. Their idea of what constitutes great amazing could be completely different from yours, and if they begin to do it consistently it could very easily damage their terrific performance.

Giving Written Feedback or 360-degree Feedback

Many people are asked for feedback on the performance of colleagues at appraisal time, either as part of a formal 360-degree feedback programme or simply in an effort to seek broader input for the performance appraisal. Often you get a form to fill in. Whether us use a form or simply write a memo or email outlining your feedback, it's important to give objective, useful information. Here's how to do it.

- ◆ Respond promptly. It is your responsibility to give accurate and honest feedback. Make sure you fulfil that responsibility even in awkward situations. It's very hard for managers to deal with difficult situations when people don't give feedback.

- ◆ If the request is very general: 'What do you think of Andrew?' or a request simply for 'feedback' ask for some specifics. Is the feedback around a particular objective? Is it around a specific incident or project? Is it about aspects of his behaviour?

- ◆ Use the same format as for spoken feedback:

➢ Focus on the facts – what happened/what the individual did: John provided all the information that we asked for within the agreed time scales. It was all accurate. We asked for the information to be provided in a table format and we got a report. Tina delivered the programme one week early and below budget.

➢ Address the results, state the impact of the action: "This meant it took as two days to identify the specific information we needed. As a result we were able to make some extra improvements."

➢ Give your praise or express your feelings, if appropriate, using concrete, specific terms. In written feedback for formal performance appraisals this is not always appropriate and it is generally best to stick to the facts, especially where there are problems. However, if it is appropriate here are some examples of effective phrasing for this kind of feedback:

- "We were delighted with the improvements."

- "We are very pleased with the service."

- "We are frustrated with the situation."

- "What would you like them to do next time?"

◆ Make any suggestions for how things could be improved next time:

➢ "It would be helpful to have the information tabulated in future."

➢ "We will be very pleased if Tina can continue this level of service. If she can give us an accurate forecast of savings a month before hand that would be a give us an opportunity to plan our spending."

- Do not make sweeping generalisations:

  - "John has been great and provides us with an excellent service."

  - "John has been useless; we never get what we need."

Statements like these make it very hard for the individual or the manager to know what you are talking about and to make the improvements and changes you need.

Getting Feedback From Others

Asking for feedback from others can be easy for some people, but it can also be quite difficult or embarrassing for some. Here are some tips to make it easier to do and enable you to get more effective results.

- Ask for feedback on your own performance. Not many people give it spontaneously, and when they do it is often because things have gone wrong.

- Make sure that people in your team ask for feedback.

- Ask for feedback in a way that makes it easy for the person you are asking.

- Be specific on what you are asking for feedback about. "We are now half way through this project..." "Yesterday you received the report..." "You have now had the first delivery..." "How are things going?"

- Check if the original objectives have been met. "Are we where you expect to be on the plan?" "Did it meet the agreed requirements?" "Was it as you ordered it?"

- Ask for suggestions on:

  - What you could have done better

➢ What you could have done more of

➢ What else you could have done

➢ What they would like you to do next time.

This makes it easy for the person giving you feedback and does not cause embarrassment.

◆ Do not ask:

➢ "What did I do wrong?"

➢ "What don't you like about me?"

➢ "What do you hate?"

This generally makes it difficult for the other person to give you useful information. Alternatively you could end up with an avalanche of abuse that could be quite depressing and de-motivating.

Feedback That Is Critical ... You may receive unwanted, unfair or unpleasant feedback that is very difficult to deal with, such as

➢ "You are useless/an idiot."

➢ "This is hopeless."

➢ "You have failed."

These statements are opinions, not facts. Here are some ideas on how to handle this type of feedback:

◆ Keep calm. Ask one of these questions (or modify to suit):

➢ "What have I done that gives you this impression?"

➢ "What has happened to make you think XXXX?"

- If the individual has nothing to back up his or her opinion, tell them that you are concerned and would be grateful if they would let you know if it happens again. Ask for some specific feedback next time on whatever you did that made them think that.

- If the individual gives you some facts that back up their opinion, and it's true, admit your error.

- Apologise if it's appropriate.

- Find out what they would like you to do differently next time.

- If the individual is in error, ask questions rather than getting into an argument or being defensive.

- Ask the person to clarify what they mean. Often people are giving opinions instead of judging your performance using the appropriate criteria.

Consider the next few examples of dialogue that could take place between you and the individual giving you feedback as a way to respond to opinion-based feedback:

- Other: "You are weak." (Opinion)

- You: "What is it you need me to achieve?" (Exhibiting Adult-based behaviour draws the other person back to your performance with this response.)

- Make sure you ask questions around this rather than how you behave.

OR

- Other: "You should be more forceful." (Opinion on how you should behave; not objective view on what has been achieved)

- You: "Which objectives do you think I have not achieved?"

Complimentary feedback ... On the other hand, you may receive feedback that praises you and your achievements.

If the feedback is well-given and specific:

- ◆ Thank the other person.

- ◆ Give your feelings

- ◆ Say what you will do next time (if appropriate).

Getting complimentary, positive feedback, for some people, can be almost as daunting as receiving criticism and unfair feedback. Here is some dialogue that presents a positive and very Lemon way to handle it.

- ◆ "Thank you. I am pleased that you are happy with the output. I will do my best to make sure it continues that way."

- ◆ "Thank you. It's very helpful to know what works for you. I'll make sure that you get the plan in advance next time too."

On the other hand, if the feedback is vague, it may be nice to hear but not give you anything to go on in terms of continuing your current successful patterns of action and interaction, such as: "That's great. Your contributions were excellent." Turn this around into something meaningful by asking for some more detail. Be specific in the way you phrase your request for more information so you will be able to create an actionable context around what the individual is trying to tell you. For example you could say this:

- ◆ "What in particular was helpful?"

- ◆ "Which contributions were of most benefit?"

In this way you will learn quickly and easily what you can do to improve and what you can do to continue taking the positive actions that earned you the praise of this individual.

There are a number of specific phrases that will be successful in eliciting a more meaningful description of what is working for the other person. Check out the following lists.

General Fact-finding Questions and Phrases:

- What happened when....?

- What did you say?

- What did you do?

- What did they say?

- What did you do then?

In referring to a particular situation, you might have this conversation:

- Do you remember the meeting with Tim yesterday?

- Do you remember what you said to Tim?

- What did he say?

- What happened?

- What was his body language?

Regarding a specific business issue:

- How many did you sell in October?

- What was the result? What was your original plan?

- How did you decide on that course of action?

- What were the overall sales?

When you have a specific problem on which you need to get feedback from your team and those involved:

- ◆ How did the team members respond to the problems?

- ◆ Did you ask them for their feedback?

- ◆ What did they say to you?

- ◆ What did the customer order?

- ◆ What did they receive?

- ◆ When did they receive what they had asked for?

- ◆ How did that happen?

And, if something goes well and you want to pinpoint to success factors for that team and event:

- ◆ What did you do that was instrumental in achieving this (objective)?

- ◆ What did you do differently this time?

- ◆ What else do you think you did that could have impacted on this objective/result?

- ◆ Did you prepare for the meeting?

- ◆ What was the effect compared to the previous time?

- ◆ How did you find out there was a problem?

- ◆ Did you tell anyone?

- ◆ When did you tell them?

- ◆ What were the consequences?

Questions relating to the **impact**

- What was the result?

- What was the impact?

- How do you think that looked to Joe?

- How do you think this makes the department look?

Dealing with **feelings** about an event or a relationship:

- How do you think I feel about this?

- How do you think he felt about that?

- How did he (she) feel about that?

Addressing the **future** ... how to handle things and improve achievement levels:

- What have you learned?

- What will you do next time?

- Where else could this help?

- What was it you wanted to achieve?

- How do you think you could achieve it next time?

- What will you do next time?

- How could what you have learned be used to help the rest of the team?

- What could you do differently next time?

- What skills do you think you need to improve on?

Appraisal Skills — Staying Objective In Your Adult Style

Conducting performance appraisals take both the right attitude and the right approach. Primarily you should make sure you are clear about what the appraisal is supposed to achieve. In most circumstances performance appraisals are used to meet the needs of the organisation and the individual in two areas: review of the individual's performance against objectives of the year that has just ended and make plans, set objectives and objectives, for the next year.

Conducting a performance appraisal is no time for a managers Parental-mode to come to the forefront. It is difficult for managers to be objective, fair and even-handed when they are viewing the situation through the eyes of the Parent persona. The very aspect of the Parent will put them in the Tell and Do mode, which leads to an appraisal that looks very much like an instructional session detailing the ways in which the individual must change their actions and/or behaviours to achieve their objectives. The Adult mode of operation is a must for managers conducting appraisals. A performance discussion is one of the most appropriate times for a manager to do some coaching with the employee. It is an effective way to address both the areas in which the person excels and the aspects in which more effort or a change of focus will yield greater success.

Appraisals and Mutual Needs of Employee and Organisation

In a Lemon organisation, the needs of the organisation and the needs of the individual will coincide and the intent behind conducting the appraisal will be synchronous. Let's take a look at both sides of the equation.

Organisational needs: Organisational needs fall into the category of what will promote the objectives of the team, department and company. Ideally, as you will find in a Lemon organisation, there will be sets of objectives that align with each other, and flow down to the individual level, so the effort the individual has been expending during the year meets not only their personal professional development objectives, but also relates to and supports the organisational objectives.

Keys to identifying and measuring against **organisational needs** include:

- ◆ Make sure the organisational objectives for the next year are going to be achieved.

- ◆ Identify actions required to ensure the objectives are met including any necessary plans for development.

- ◆ Make appropriate decisions on pay rises and bonuses for the performance and achievements in the previous year. (Pay is not linked to appraisals in every organisation.) In organisations where there is a link between pay and performance, the appraisal results are one of several inputs. The decision is rarely the manager's alone. Make sure you are clear what the procedure is in your own organisation.

In Lemon companies, the needs of the organisation and the needs of the individual will be synchronous.

Individual's needs: Agree what has been achieved in the previous year and to what standard, in a fair and open manner.

- ◆ Understand what the department/organisation needs to achieve in the next year and the individual's personal role, contribution and responsibility.

- ◆ Be clear how they will know if they are doing it and what the measures are.

- ◆ Agree on what help they can get from others.

- ◆ Identify what resources are available to them.

- ◆ Find out what career-development opportunities are realistically available to them.

- ◆ Identify and agree on future development actions.

The whole process: Make sure you understand how the appraisal system fits into the performance management system in your organisation. In most cases it is not a stand-alone procedure.

Planning for the appraisal: If your appraisal system is linked to pay or bonuses, make sure you understand exactly what this link is and what information is required for this to be done properly and fairly.

Check you have all the relevant paperwork ready. This could include:

1. 360 degree feedback

2. Copies of the objectives from last year

3. Records and notes about what has been achieved

4. Interim review paperwork

5. Development plan

Make sure you and the person whose review you will be conducting each have copies of all the relevant paperwork several days beforehand. This should ensure each person knows what is likely to come up so you both can come to the discussion properly prepared. Check your notes on achievements during the year. In addition to these advance actions, ask your direct report to identify areas of development he is interested in. Ask him to take the initiative to find out about opportunities and let you know where his interests are focussed before the appraisal. Identify possible career development opportunities for the individual and collect the details, such as job descriptions and person specifications so you can have them to hand in the appraisal. Ask the individual to prepare draft objectives for the next year, if that is part of your system.

Besides ensuring all the documentation that you and your direct report will need during the appraisal discussion is available, your preparation should include the following items or activities:

1. Check you are clear about the paperwork procedures you need to follow including:

   ➢ What notes need to be made

   ➢ Who signs what

   ➢ Who keeps a copy of what

   ➢ Who is given a copy of what

   ➢ The appropriate deadlines for each stage of the procedure

2. Agree with the individual on a suitable date, time and agenda for the appraisal well in advance (at least one week).

3. Book a suitable room for the interview. In many companies there is a shortage of available rooms, especially at appraisal time. Make sure you have a room booked in good time.

4. Make sure the room is in a location where the individual is likely to feel comfortable and is arranged in a way that is relaxed, not threatening.

5. Turn off your mobile phone.

6. Divert your desk phone to ensure there are no interruptions if you have to do the session in your office.

7. Ensure you have allowed enough time for the meeting, but be prepared to reconvene to complete the discussion if necessary.

8. Do your best to ensure that nothing in the appraisal comes as a surprise to the individual. If it does you have failed during the year in your duties as a manager. Make sure you tackle problems and give appropriate feedback all through the year. Don't hoard it all for the appraisal.

9. Review objectives regularly during the year. Research shows that employees who believe their managers know what they have been doing during the year perform substantially better than those who don't.

10. Focus on what has been achieved and done well. Make sure you find out what the person has achieved related to the objectives. Identify what their specific contribution was.

11. Talk to colleagues and customers (both internal and external) to find out what the individual has achieved and how it has been done.

12. Encourage your direct report to keep records of what she has achieved as she goes through the year. It's a good idea to put notes at regular intervals in her diary to remind her to do this. Many people forget all the good things they did at the beginning of the year and remember only the problems and mistakes near the end of the year. Help her make sure she gets credit for all the good stuff.

13. Update the objectives through the year. Business needs change and so do priorities. When an objective becomes irrelevant note the date and reason. As new objectives are generated add them to the list.

14. Have regular informal reviews of progress so that you know whether the objectives have been achieved or not, and whether you are giving the necessary support your direct report needs to be successful.

Structure of the appraisal interview. Stick to the same structure you would use for any meeting:

> ➢ **Introduction**

1. Explain to the person what is going to happen during the appraisal and give them an idea of how long it is likely to take.

2. Never start with questions like "How's it been going?" or "How do you think the year has gone?" These questions are asking for an opinion. If that opinion is different from yours, you will have created an unnecessary argument before you have even started. Appraisals are about facts and objective measurements, not opinions. If you must ask a general question, keep it to social topics.

3. Begin by explaining the structure, what will happen and how long it is likely to take. Agree exactly what you expect as the outcome of the appraisal. This will probably include some kind of performance rating, a set of objectives and a development plan.

4. Agree who is responsible for what during the meeting. For instance: Who will be taking notes? Who will write it up? Are you each responsible for telling the other if you don't agree? Are you responsible for checking the notes to make sure they are what you agreed? If you can't agree, check the organisation procedure on this. Actually, you need to have checked on what is the standard organisational procedure for this before you begin the appraisal. It will look as if you are not prepared if you have to check after the appraisal has started.

> ➢ **Main body**

1. Review the past year including: the objectives, and what was achieved; and the development plan, and what happened and what was achieved

➤ Ask the individual which objective he would like to review first. It's his appraisal, not yours. If he is particularly worried about a specific problem, he may want to get it over with immediately or he may want to leave it till last. Let him choose.

➤ Take each objective in turn. Check the individual's understanding of the measure for that objective by asking questions:

✗ What were the measures for this objective?

✗ When was the deadline?

✗ What was important about how this objective was achieved?

✗ Check what really happened from the individual's perspective (You should already have plenty of information yourself on this from your preparation before hand.) Ask questions like:

• What happened?

• When was it achieved?

✗ Find out if the measures were met. Do this by asking questions. In most cases you will already know this from your reviews during the year.

2. Agree on objectives for the next year

✗ Make sure the objectives are both clear and **measurable.** Clear objectives have a direct effect on a person's performance. The clearer they are, the more likely the individual is to achieve them. They need to include

- Exactly what it is that needs to be achieved.

- A measure, so you will both be clear whether it has been achieved or not.

- A time limit or deadline.

× Make sure all the objectives are relevant to the overall organisational objectives and contribute to the objectives of your team.

× Make sure the objective is possible and the individual has the resources and authority they need in order to get it done.

× Be open-minded about the objectives that are going to be agreed. If your organisation has a system where the manager sets the objectives, you might also find it worthwhile to ask for the individual's thoughts on them.

× Check how the individual expects to achieve the objectives. Ask them how they plan to go about achieving the objective. This will give you a good idea of their level of understanding and skill.

× Note down any skills they will need to learn in order to achieve the objectives.

× Explain that the objectives may need to be updated through the year, if that is appropriate.

× Check the individual understands how their performance will be measured. Understanding of performance measures greatly improves performance.

× If you can't measure the objective then it probably is not a well-written, clear objective and you need to go back to it and ask yourself exactly what needs to be achieved.

× Prioritise your objectives: If you have this system, make sure you use it. It is very important that an individual knows and understands the relevant priorities of each objective. This helps them to make decisions in their day-to-day work. Stating that all objectives are priority 1 implies that you, as the manager, can't prioritise.

× Some systems ask you to indicate a percentage of time estimated for each objective. Use it if it's there. This information can be very helpful as it gives a person a good idea how long a task should take and helps them to know if they are going off track; a very useful warning system if used properly.

3. Ask the individual to define his long term career aspirations

× Check if there are specific opportunities that the individual might be interested in.

× If there are specific roles the individual would like to aim for, use the person specification and job description to identify the skills that need to be developed. You can do this by looking for examples of things they have achieved to see if the individual's skills match the requirements.

× If there are new areas the person is interested in, identify the skills they already have and the new ones that would be required.

× Gather together the development needs you have noted during the other parts of the appraisal and sort them into skill areas.

× Identify in each skill exactly what the individual needs to be able to do once the skill has been mastered. Write this as the objective. For example: be *able to operate the XYZ machine so that it produces 60 units per hour that meet the quality standards, or be able to prepare and give a ten-minute presentation of the month's sales figures for the board.*

4. Create a development plan (using information from the review, objectives for the next year and career plans)

   × Identify together how the skills can be learned after you have agreed what they are. There are many possible routes. They include:

   • Training course

   • Coaching

   • Mentoring

   • Reading up on the subject

   • Training videos

   • E-learning

   • Shadowing skilled colleagues

   • Job rotation

- Secondment

- Asking someone else who knows how to do it

x Work out a plan including measures

x Do not agree for the individual to *go on XXXX training course* as a development objective. Make sure you are clear what needs to be learned, any action the individual takes to achieve that will be much more effective. The objective should be around what the individual needs to be able to do as a result of the training or other action.

x You might need to remind the individual that sometimes, although she would like to develop in specific areas, those areas may not be relevant to the work she does, or there just may not be the budget for it. However, if it is possible to apply flexibility, allow the individual to negotiate in these situations.

x Be honest. Say *No* if necessary. Not all development is going to help the organisation directly. However, bear in mind that learning new things and improving their skills motivates many people. If you do not have the budget, say so. If you can't see how the development could be relevant, ask the individual how they think it will help. If it does not fit in with the organisation's plans, say so.

x Ask the individual about any other areas in which she is interested. This could include jobs she would like to be considered for, departments she would like to work in or projects she would find challenging.

➢ Summary

1. Explain, clarify and discuss the scores, grades and ratings *(Not applicable to all organisations)*

2. Make sure you understand the criteria for making these decisions. It's useful to have some examples of each level. If you are not sure, check.

3. Make sure you can explain to the person the decisions you make in this area in terms of the agreed criteria your organisation uses.

4. Then be ready to explain:

    × "The criteria for classifying an objective as 'B' are that it has been met within the time agreed and within budget. This objective was one week late in being achieved so the performance rating must be below 'B'."

    × People are much better motivated when these systems have clear criteria and are fairly applied.

    × Another way to do this is to ask the person to work it out themselves: *What do you understand as* the criteria for a 'B' on any one objective? Were those met in *this case?* This method is usually easier and more effective.

> **In an appraisal you are always grading the individual's performance, NOT the individual.**

Remember that you are grading the performance, not the person. Use phrases like *your achievements here* can be rated as... Never use: <u>*you are rated as...*</u> This can be offensive and also ultimately reduces performance as you are in effect telling the person they are their rating rather than their performance is rated at a certain level.

- Make sure the person understands what they need to do differently in order to achieve a higher rating or grade next time. This is one of the key ways to improve a person's performance. It's one of the most powerful tools in your hands – so use it. Identify training needs and make a note of them for later in the appraisal.

- Be realistic in your expectations – not everyone is a superstar.

- Make sure you are clear in stating exactly what the person needs to do differently next time in order to improve any ratings or grades. If you are not clear about the ratings tell the person you are meeting with that you will find out and arrange a discussion in the future. However, by going into the performance appraisal unprepared — this would definitely signal that you are unprepared and haven't gotten the ratings and requirements clear in your own mind before conducting the appraisal — you send two messages to the individual: first, that you haven't taken your role as manager seriously, and second, that don't care enough about that person to find out everything you need to know in advance. Lemon managers do not let this happen to themselves.

- Go into the appraisal open-minded. Do not make your decision on any grade or rating before you have carried out the appraisal. Otherwise the appraisal is meaningless. Rather than being an honest appraisal, it becomes a reporting session where you are telling the individual your predetermined opinions about their performance.

- Make sure that your decisions on any grades you will be giving are consistent with other employees and other departments. (The emphasis here is <u>consistent</u>, not the <u>same</u>.) You can do this by checking with your own manager, HR people and often, through material your organisation provides.

- Ask the individual to summarise the key points that have been agreed. This is likely to include

- × An overall view of what has been achieved, including any threads that have become apparent

- × A brief summary of the objectives that have been agreed

- × A summary of the development actions

- × The actions the manager will take

- × The actions the individual will take

- Sign the relevant documents or agree who will write these up and when they will be signed, depending on your system.

- Thank the individual for their efforts

Tips for conducting the appraisal itself

1. Help the individual to feel relaxed. This can be more difficult than it sounds. People are generally nervous if they don't know what is coming or they are convinced it is going to be bad.

2. Nothing should ever come to the individual as a surprise in an appraisal. If it does, you have failed in your management responsibilities. You need to deal with problems and issues as they arise, not leave them till the appraisal. The appraisal is a summary just like the year-end accounts of a company.

3. If appropriate, get coffees or some other drink. Walking to a drinks machine can help a person to calm down.

4. Give the individual choice at every opportunity. People feel more stressed when they feel out of control. This could be as simple as

asking them where they would like to sit, or if they would like a drink now or later.

5.   You may want to consider starting with some small talk. Be aware that some people will see this as the dentist rearranging the surgical implements before pulling the tooth. Others will find it relaxing.

FAQs

1.   *What if they think they have achieved the objective and I don't think they have?* First check how clear the objective is and the measures are. Ask the individual for his understanding of both. If his understanding is different than yours, then you need to apologise that it wasn't clear in the first place. You can't mark someone down for having achieved the wrong objective if you (or another manager) agreed on it with him in the first place.

2.   *I think he's done badly and he thinks he's done well. What do I do?* You need to stick to facts rather than opinions. *Badly* is an opinion, not a fact. Stick to the questions about what the objectives and measures were and what actually happened. Make sure you both understand the measures. Keep the discussion around what happened and away from judgements.

3.   *What do I do when I have a very quiet person who will hardly say anything?* Keep quiet yourself. I once had to wait five minutes for an answer, but it was worth it. When someone is very quiet, the temptation is to start talking yourself or to ask another question. This generally makes things worse for that person. So just ask your question and then wait.

4.   *What about people who talk a lot? How do I keep them on track?* Summarise what they say and then move on to the next topic: *So the objective was achieved on time but went £3000 over budget ... or ... What happened to the ABC report?* Summarising will show you

have listened and understood. Asking the question will move them on to the next area for discussion. In really difficult cases, use their name to focus their attention.

5. *What if we can't agree on whether an objective has been achieved or not?* In this case it is likely that the objective, the measure or both were unclear or written in a way that was open to interpretation. At this stage it's too late to update the objective now. As the manager, your best option is to apologise for the misunderstanding and make sure that, next time, it is clear. For the current appraisal, you will have to go with the individual's interpretation of the objective and measures.

6. *How do I make appraisals become part of daily life rather than an annual chore for both parties?* Set regular dates to review progress towards objectives and to update them as necessary. Get the individual to note the progress as you go along. Use the same kinds of questions as I suggest for the appraisals themselves: What has happened? What have you achieved so far? In other words, have regular coaching sessions and use the objectives as your starting point.

7. *How do I avoid increasing bureaucracy if I have these regular coaching review sessions?* All you need to do is keep notes of achievements as you go along – you can do this live during the session if you like. Also ask the individual to note all their achievements either on the appraisal form as they go or separately for reference later. This will reduce the time and effort you have to spend searching for records and trying to remember what happened during the year when it comes to the appraisal itself. Additionally, you could ask the individual to send you an email summarising the completion of the project or objective and highlighting their achievements against the applicable objective.

8. *How do you carry out the appraisal of someone who was originally a friend or peer and you are now his or her manager?* If you stick to asking questions rather than telling the person, you will find this much easier. Ask questions to clarify the facts. Then if you have to grade the performance, get the individual to explain their understanding of the rating system and the criteria for making that decision. Then ask them to make the decision using those criteria. The whole point of having clear criteria is to make these decisions transparent. Once again, if that individual has good, measurable objectives written in the first place, the process of reviewing performance will be easily focussed on the actions rather than the individual.

9. *How do I deal with a manager who won't listen to the facts?* You need to find out from the manager what his/her criteria are for making the judgements they have made. Do this by asking questions, (not telling them): What were the measures for this objective? What was the actual expenditure? So are you saying that, although the *budget was met, that the objective was not met?* Asking questions is always more effective than telling. Another key is to make sure the objectives and measures are crystal clear in the first place and the individual knows exactly how his performance is going to be measured.

10. *How do I avoid focusing on recent history at the expense of earlier behaviour?* Keeping regular notes through the year will do that for you. If you have trouble remembering, put reminders in your diary. Update your notes on an individual's performance at least once a month.

11. *How do we make this process motivational instead of the opposite?* Make sure you concentrate on what the person has achieved and what she needs to do next time to improve her performance. Have a plan of action by the end of the discussion, including a development plan. Do not focus on weaknesses, character flaws and

failures as, not only is this de-motivating, but research shows it actually reduces a person's level of performance.

12. *What do I do if the individual bursts into tears?* Here are some options. Choose the one that you feel is the most appropriate in the circumstances. Most importantly, make it clear that the process will continue, even if it will be delayed.

   ◆ Wait till the tears stop and carry on

   ◆ Ask if they would like to take a short break

   ◆ Ask if they would like to continue on a separate day

   ◆ Get them to move physically (stand up, walk to the coffee machine) as this can help a person to feel calmer. If you think tears are likely have some tissues ready!

Feedback For The Manager and Organisation

Provide an opportunity to the individual to make comments and suggestions. Getting your direct report's feedback can be very instructive and beneficial both for you and for the future of the organisation. Looked at it objectively — the comments can tell you a great deal about the kind of organisation you have, how it could be made better, and what might be occurring within it that could be detrimental to becoming or staying a Lemon company.

Getting feedback from a subordinate can be instructive and valuable to the future of the manager and to the organisation.

To elicit feedback from your direct report, ask questions like:

◆ What could I do to make it easier for you to achieve your objectives? Or What could the organisation do to be more effective?

◆ Ask the individual to give you feedback on what you can do to make things easier for him.

◆ Use this format: *In XXX situation how well did action YYY work for you and the team, and what could have made it better?* This is much easier for the individual to do than tell you what she wants you to stop doing and is usually much more effective.

Communication — Managing Your Delivery, Filtered Through Adult Intention

Communication is the universal glue that pulls together all the aspects of managing and coaching. The varied ways in which managers interact with their direct reports are all grounded in the communication methods they use ... and which have been reinforced for them through their own professional maturity and development. An Adult communication mode is, of course, the optimal business communication method because it yields the most positive and productive results. In fact, Adult communication includes both the words used and the manner in which they are spoken: the words they choose indicate inclusiveness, support, acceptance and open-mindedness, as well as the tone and body language that are consistent with the words. What this means in a business environment is that Adult communication invites discussion, demonstrates that the speaker is not judging the other as a person, encourages initiative on the part of the other person, and expresses opinions in a non-threatening manner.

Contrasted with Adult communication, Parental communication is directive, sometimes threatening, sometimes dismissive, and can sound cold and unfeeling, especially when coupled with the typical vocal intonation and body language that accompanies a manager in Parent mode giving instruction, direction and criticism. Why is all this important? It is important because communication is the conduit for all of these management techniques to be construed by the direct report in either a constructive and supportive manner or a rejecting and disapproving one.

There is little point to communication if it doesn't move people to action.

The purpose of most communication occurring within organisations is to move people to action of one kind or another. Adults communicate in an open way, using objective language that is neither threatening nor so neutral it comes across as uninterested. Their communication fosters greater understanding and heightened awareness between themselves and those with whom they interact. It also stimulates a correspondingly non-threatening response from the other person.

Communication Styles

Communication is, by definition, an interchange of information, thoughts or opinions by means of speech, writing or signs. Communication style is a term that refers to the manner in which individuals communicate with others and includes:

- The way they share information (freely, reluctantly)

- The way they receive information (openly, resentfully, sceptically)

- The language they use (formal, informal, stilted, vernacular)

- The style and manner of speaking that is predominant in their everyday contact with others (open, obtuse, friendly, harsh, abusive, tentative)

- Their intent (to share, to instruct, to inform, to validate, to chastise, to uplift, to humiliate)

- The body language they use when they speak (crossed arms, open stance, hands on hips, non-threatening stance)

- The communication method (face-to-face, in writing, telephone) they prefer

Most of us use a variety of communication methods and approaches, and have more than one manner of speaking and way of giving and receiving communication. Most of us also have preferred or more prevalent methods, approaches and manners, and that can tell us a lot about the kind of person they are because who you are is very much reflected in the way you communicate. For example, take our

Communication only occurs when an exchange of thoughts results in shared understanding.

typical Parent-mode, Monkey manager illustrated so often in this book. This individual will most frequently be seen as the type of communicator who:

- Seldom shares information, and then very reluctantly

- Receives information most often sceptically, and sometimes resentfully

- Often communicates in a very formal manner, maintaining the instructional, Parental attitude

- Uses harsh speech, which sometimes borders on or becomes abusive

- Most often communicates to inform and to instruct, sometimes to chastise or humiliate

- Uses closed or aggressive body language with crossed arms and hands on hips

- Prefers written communication and will use face-to-face as a last resort

Contrast those characteristics with what we know about Lemon managers who are able to communicate in Adult mode. You will most often see them a communicator who:

- Shares information regularly, knowing that colleagues and direct reports need to be kept informed to be able to do their jobs well

- Receives information openly, and invites communication by the way they receive it

- Uses informal but clear language when communicating in writing or speaking

- Has a manner of speaking that is open and friendly, inclusive and respectful

- Communicates for the purpose of sharing knowledge and information, uplifting the receiver (is continually in a positive coaching role), and validating another's approach as well as accomplishments

- Uses an open, non-threatening stance in face-to-face encounters ... doesn't feel the need to close up and adopt a protective stance

- Prefers face-to-face communication but is comfortable with all methods and uses them appropriately

It's not hard to determine which management communication style you would rather face in the person you work for, and which one is the most likely to cultivate more Lemons. The positive always outweighs the negative, and just looking at the differences in styles speaks volumes about the kind of organisation the two communication styles would foster. You may have noticed that the Parent mode that keeps coming up in examples within the book is the harsher, more judgmental parent, and you would be right. I have found that rather than the nurturing parent who strives to do the best for their children by guarding them from making bad decisions, the one who shows up in business most often is the judgmental authoritarian, who feels compelled to correct the misbehaviour of direct reports at every possible opportunity. Truly, guarding your employees from making bad decisions is no more constructive than yanking projects away from them because you are impatient with their actions, but that is more often the judging Parent that shows up in a monkey-filled business environment ... the autocratic, judgmental, instructive parent who is determined to whip their direct reports into shape, even if it kills them. Sadly, it often does — at least it often kills their self-confidence and self-respect.

Communication in writing can be a wonderful or a terrible thing. A person's communication style clearly is reflected in the way they write, both in the words they use and the way they structure their writing. Angry written communication has an aspect even more potentially damaging than spoken communication ... it is permanent! Printed communication has the indelible memory of the proverbial elephant, and you can't ever take it back! Worse yet, it can be shared with another at any point in time, over and over again.

Most managers learn never to put angry thoughts in writing — or at least never to send them out to the recipient. They should remain locked in the bottom drawer until the fit of anger is over, and then they should be put through the shredder. Unfortunately, many managers locked in the Monkey Syndrome don't have the time, or the inclination, to edit themselves and never stop to consider the impact of their words in either a verbal or written context. Good Lemon managers also find themselves dealing with written diatribes, which in today's age of technology often arrive in the form of the "email from hell." You know, the ones written in caps so you can tell the writer is SCREAMING. We've probably all received at least one from some hapless (e.g. stupid) individual who hit "send" before he engaged his brain and is now kicking himself around the office wishing to heaven he could take back what he just "said." And worst of all, not only is such an email now permanent, it is also floating out there in cyberspace for virtually anyone to see... even the discretion of the receiver won't protect the careless sender from someone else intercepting it. The possibilities for this indiscretion hitting the fan are endless and awful. If the imprudent sender is a manager, he has, at the least, made an intensely career-limiting move. At the worst, in the wrong hands and depending on the content, this could mean the end of his career at that company. And it is much more likely to happen to a Monkey manager in full Parent mode because he is so focussed on making his point and correcting the behaviour of a direct report who has transgressed that he seldom stops to think about either the appropriateness of this kind of response or the ramifications of it on both the individual and himself.

Understanding Communication Styles

Because communication is such a key element of interaction within organisations — indeed, it is the conduit for all types of organisational transactions — it is a self-aware manager who recognises his own style and who also realises that it is important to be able to recognise the style used by others, from his bosses to his direct reports. To understand others, it is easier to start with yourself; it is even essential, because with self-knowledge comes the perspective that will enable him to recognise those with like styles and those whose styles are inconsistent or in conflict with his own. In turn, that knowledge will make him a more effective communication.

Signals of a person's communication style are sent in a variety of means. One obvious way is to look at their most prevalent (and apparently preferred) method, approach and language. To help define someone's style, consider this:

- Does she send more emails or make more phone calls? Does she respond quickly to an email message, or does she just ignore them? Does she always answer the phone, or do you inevitably get bounced into voice mail?

- Is she relaxed and open when conversing in person? Or is she nervous and closed-off, with folded arms?

- Is her language informal, casual and colloquial? Is her speech appropriate to the situation: casual when speaking with friends and colleagues in an informal setting and more formal when speaking before a group or with her superiors? Or does she speak precisely and formally in even casual encounters?

Few people behave only one way all of the time, but you can get the gist of someone's communication style by observing the way they interact with you and others over time. If you observe that their communication style is flexible and appropriate to the circumstances, you have found someone who is self-confident and able to be authentic ... probably a self-aware Lemon.

Right Brain — Left Brain

How a person communicates also is an indication of how they think, and vice versa. You've likely heard people referred to as either 'right brained' or 'left brained.' These labels refer to something called hemispheric dominance ... meaning that one or the other of the primary hemispheres of the brain is predominant, signified by the way in which people learn and their preferences in a variety of activities, including communication. There are no absolutes here and both hemispheres of the brain are involved in just about every human activity. However, brain research has confirmed that people for whom the left side of the brain is dominant tend to process information in a linear, sequential and structured manner. They are often described as analytical and methodical, less emotional, and, sometimes, coldly logical. Their learning style is demonstrated by what is called a Reflector or Theorist learning style — they will want to see an agenda, they like logic sequencing and detail, and they will be organized and methodical. They often work from A to Z.

Left brain dominance indicates a predisposition to linear, analytical, logical thinking.

On the other hand, those for whom the right side of the brain appears dominant tend to process information in a more random, imagistic and holistic manner; and are said to be more visual, intuitive, and emotional. Their right brain dominance is demonstrate by an Activist or Pragmatist learning style — they will like pictures and mindmaps, many are doodlers, and they will respond to humour and may be animated people. They often work from Z to A.

Research has shown that some people can be left brain thinkers and display right brain behaviour, and vice versa. However, most of the time, the way you think and the way you behave are synchronised; that is, right brain thinking is paired with right brain behaviour. What we are looking at is dominance ... majority use. In some cases, we find extremely left or right brained examples of behaviour. An easy, well-known example of left brained thinking and behaviour is Spock from Star Trek ... easily identified as a clear example of someone (albeit a fictitious someone) with a hugely unemotional and logical personality. And you may come across an extreme right brainer ... take any entertainer coming out of Hollywood ... who is random, very visual and has extravagantly animated body language. In most cases, people operate near the centre point.

Right brain dominance is manifested in a learning style that is visual, intuitive, random and imagistic.

Experts point out that you can spot a left or right 'brainer' by observing their body language. Left brainers are said to be stiller, use less personal space and are generally quieter, whereas right brainers are animated in their body language, more extroverted and are often in need of visual stimulation. While there is no absolute proof of this, one could interpret the "signs" in a business setting. Left brainers may take up less space in a meeting room or on a meeting table, often having the folders, pens and diary in perfect linear rows, whereas right brainers "land grab" and throw their stuff into all four corners of their allotted space without care to such pointless need for order. In other words, brain dominance influences body language, and body language is one aspect of an individual's communication style.

Why are these left brain – right brain concepts pertinent to communication? Because when a left brainer (one who tends to be more reserved, logical and methodical) meets a right brainer (one who is more open, outgoing and random) there is an excellent opportunity for communication to break down between them. Grasping the left brain – right brain context, and the functional differences between the two predominant patterns of behaviour, is the first step in becoming more flexible in your communication style. Key to this is to realise that the reason why certain people can't understand others is because of these differences. Each is pushing the communication buttons from their own brain dominance (preferred styles). Common mistakes that lead to miscommunication would include:

- A left brainer (who likes detail, logical proposals and conversation) taking an eternity to get to their point whilst talking to an impatient right brainer

- A right brainer who just wants to get the job done and has an idea or a plan – attempts to enlist his left brained team members by explaining it in a high level superficial way, using enthusiasm and extroversion to gain their attention and buy in

- Both can cause immense frustration and sometimes dislike of each other ... leading to one or the other being labelled "difficult people"

- Sometimes the reason someone is seen as difficult or hard to communicate with is simply because they are *different* – not actually difficult.

Written communication apparently is also affected by brain dominance: right brainers write email, for example, in a superficial one line or a mostly bulleted and pointed fashion, whereas left brainers typically right more "blocky" paragraph formatted text, and expand their points beyond a few words. Right brainers write fewer notes; while left brainers write notes and lists about lists. Body language give-aways are also good indicators of communication style and there are some that relate to brain dominance.

- Right brainers pace around – whilst on the telephone especially

- Right brainers usually are poorer time managers than left brainers (order, logic and a Be Perfect driver being absent) – effort from the right brainer can counter this, we are talking natural flair again (we can all learn techniques to counter dominance)

◆ Left brainers are usually better listeners – as they are not as easily distracted (visual stimuli across the office or the thought process of "just hurry the hell up" disrupts a right brainers ability to listen as well, at least without exercising effort)

So, the bottom line is that knowing and understanding yourself — your behaviour and communication style — can help you do two things: first, identify the style of the person with whom you are attempting to communicate, and second, learn to modify your own style by exercising control and self-editing speech and body language. Here's what I mean. A left brain dominant individual who tends to over-explain and give too much information verbally and who usually sends long, involved emails can learn to cut both spoken and written communication down to what is necessary for optimal understanding when they know they will be dealing with a right brained individual. Conversely, a right brainer can keep in mind that more information may be necessary to get his point across than he would typically put in a one-liner email or a two second voice mail. Both can develop the flexibility to work with each other, give consideration to each other's communication preferences and needs, and eliminate, or at least reduce, the frustration that occurs when they come head to head in a communication tangle.

Knowing and understanding your own communication style will help you identify the style of the other person and modify your own style to improve communication between you.

Communication flexibility is really essential for a manager to be a Lemon leader, and to cultivate a department full of Lemons. Picture a whole room full of people whose style is the opposite of yours, or at best a mixed bag of right, left and middle brain people who all have differing communication needs. You may have to find a good solid middle ground to capture and hold the attention of the majority. Your ability to step out of your own sphere of preference, especially if you tend to be on the extreme end of either, could spell success for you and your direct reports. Further, in a one-on-one coaching situation, understanding where your coachee is coming from will spell the difference between wasted time and truly meaningful interaction. Take any of the examples of the extremes, and apply them to the idea of coaching someone who is the opposite of you. If you, as the manager, cannot move out of your comfort zone surrounded by the familiarity of your own communication style, you will miss the critical opportunity to connect with your coachee. Putting yourself in your direct reports mental shoes and modifying your style to fit his needs is the sign of a dedicated and engaged manager. At the same time you are modifying your own style, you in turn are teaching that person successful ways to modify his.

Managing Difficult People — When Employees Act Like Children

Many people have trouble dealing with "Difficult People." This is because they don't know what to do to handle them, adjust the behaviour or deal with the chaos that they sometimes leave in their wake. In this section we cover some important tips and techniques for dealing with six different kinds of difficult behaviour.

Find Out The Facts

To diagnose and determine solutions to dealing with a difficult person, the place to start is with the facts. Look at what is really going on in order to figure out what to do about it.

To try to diagnose what makes that person difficult, ask yourself these questions:

1. What does the person do that makes him 'difficult'?

2. Is there something that you would like him to do that he is not doing? What is it?

3. Does he behave this way with everyone?

4. Does this happen with just a few people or just one person? Who?

5. What is the context for the behaviours you don't want? (For example: Is it when he is under pressure, on Mondays, dealing with certain topics?)

Once you have the facts you can start to work out what to do.

Behaviour Types

There are a number of behaviours we have all observed or experienced that would be categorized as difficult, even malevolent. Here are some typical difficult behaviours to watch out for and the outward symptoms of each.

Insensitive Behaviour

We've all made comments like "That was very insensitive of him," meaning that what the person did was very thoughtless of the feelings or needs or attitudes of another person. At its worst, it is exhibited in exceedingly deleterious ways within organisations. At its simpler levels, insensitivity can be seen simply as a very self-focussed approach to the work place.

Insensitive behaviour is exemplified by these actions:

1. **Lack of greetings and goodbyes**. This person will rarely ask how you are or how your holiday was. At the end of a conversation, they won't thank you or say how nice it was to see you.

2. **Very task-focussed behaviour.** They will be most concerned about what needs to be done and what they are doing. They will be unconcerned about the effects on other people.

3. **Lack of awareness of others' needs.** They will not ask you what you need – for example, if you would like a drink. If you don't

understand something they will often not respond with an explanation.

4. **Lack of awareness of others' emotions.** If you are concerned, cross, happy or worried their behaviour will remain the same. They will not notice how you are feeling. They will not predict how you are likely to feel as a result of what they say, nor do they appear to care.

5. **Lecturing rather than engaging in a conversation.** Most conversations are made of links. Each person builds on what the other said and links it to the subject area. These people do not link with the topics of the other person, they seem to ignore them and just continue on their own topic.

6. **Lack of embarrassment.** Most people show embarrassment when they have done something that is socially inappropriate. These people do not.

There are some specific steps you can take to modify and neutralize the behaviour of insensitive people. Here's what you can do:

1. When dealing with Insensitive Behaviour people, you need to give them *very clear* and *direct* feedback, using their name. This alone may start to change their behaviour.

2. Remember to tell them what you want them to do instead of telling them what you don't want. It's much more effective because trying to "not do" something is more difficult than substituting acceptable actions and behaviours. Make the desired actions very clear.

    ➢ Wrong - "John, I don't think the people next door want to hear what we are saying."

    ➢ Correct - "John, please lower your voice, I don't want to disturb the people in the next room."

This may feel rather awkward to you, but it will be perfectly acceptable to them. They will usually do what you say as a result.

3. Be consistent in your feedback. Random feedback is confusing and will lead to random behaviour. When the person does something you are pleased with – give clear feedback:

> ➢ Correct — "When you finished that report early it was a great help to me. It meant I had more time to prepare for my meeting."

> ➢ Wrong — "That's great, thanks."

Vague or unclear instructions will not generate a change in behaviour for insensitive people. To create a change, be clear, specific and definite in the actions and behaviours you are asking for.

4. Don't take their lack of greetings or interest in you as a personal insult. It's not meant as one. They are simply often oblivious to others or to their needs.

5. Keep your conversation to tasks at hand and what needs to be done.

6. If you want elicit a change in behaviour, be as specific as you can about what you want them to do and explain it in steps. For example, if your person is not dealing effectively with client calls:

> ➢ Correct — "When a client calls with a problem here's what I want you to do:"

> ✗ "Go into their page on the database"

> ✗ "Ask the client to explain what the problem is"

> ✗ "Ask them when it first started"

> ✗ "Ask them what they need us to do"

     ✗ "Ask them how soon they need it to be done"

     ✗ "Enter all this information into the database"

➢ Wrong — "Find out what they need." This is too vague and gives no direction as to the new behaviour you want the individual to adopt.

Theory of Insensitive People

◆ The difficulty for people who behave insensitively is that they do not understand hints; so you need to be direct. It is also likely that they will not feel embarrassment – so don't worry about that either.

◆ They aren't easily embarrassed or shamed because they do not have the sensitivity to pick up the feedback that most people hear or see easily. An insensitive person will not notice signals like a raised eyebrow, a nod or a change in intonation. (This part is just like having poor hearing or being in a room that's too dark to see anything.)

◆ Even if they did notice a feedback signal they probably would not be able to interpret it correctly. As a result of this, they have not had feedback on their behaviour in a form they can understand. Once the feedback is in a form they can understand, then it is much more likely that they will respond.

◆ The emotion of embarrassment is itself feedback. It is there to tell you that you have done something socially inappropriate. If you did not ever feel embarrassment, how would you be able to determine for yourself when you had made a mistake?

Very Detail-Oriented People

Another difficult type of individual is one who is very detail-oriented. This can be both good and bad. There has to be someone in every department and on every team that can focus on the details. At the same time, these individuals tend to overlook the big picture in their total attention to the details. Of course, this can be both aggravating and almost "anti-strategic." Behaviours identifying detail-oriented people that you should look out for include:

1. **You think you have agreed on an action with the person and it does not happen.** When you investigate they will have performed a very small part of the task, gotten stuck and gone no further.

2. **Things do not happen when you need them to happen.** You will have asked for something to be done, thinking it was obvious that it was really urgent. The person will have left the task for later.

3. **There are strange misunderstandings that only happen with that person, not with anyone else.** For example: You will have had queries from this person over one small phrase in an email or letter. Another example might be that this person will remember a conversation you had with them which appears to have had a completely different conclusion for that person than the one you remember.

4. **The person thinks they are very good at planning, but your view is different.** They are good at planning in the short term, but do not seem to think about the longer term at all.

5. **This person cannot see the big picture.** They may quibble over tiny amounts of money while not considering the annual budget. They may have the reputation of being a "nit-picker".

6. **They tend to give long answers to your questions.** They may tend to continue "waffling" when you consider the conversation should be over.

7. **They work in a step by step manner.** They like to follow a process. When there is no process, they are unhappy and lost. Some are unable to get themselves going on the project at all.

8. **They take little or no initiative.** When things change, they do not modify their approach accordingly. They rarely come up with ideas.

The steps you can take to address their behaviours and move them toward the outcomes you need are these:

1. Identify if the person ever does what you ask them to do. If you can identify instances when the person actually does what is asked of them, you will be able to determine the difference between these situations and the ones that give you trouble. Once you have the difference then you usually have a way forward.

2. Always give a deadline. Although it may seem obvious to you how urgent something is, it is not obvious to them. Words like "immediately," "urgent," "straight away" and "soon" mean different things to different people. You have to be very specific and never assume the individual will perceive the urgency without having to spell it out for them.

3. Check their understanding of the context. Make sure it's the same as yours. A person who is very detail-oriented may not be aware of the context and will therefore not be able to prioritise effectively.

> **Detail-oriented people need to receive detailed and thorough instructions and specific steps.**

4. Check how stressed the person is — the more stressed, the more difficult it is for them to prioritise and

plan. You need to give them the priorities and also let them know when the priorities change. Don't expect them to just "know."

5. Ask for their plan whenever you ask them to do something. This will give you a good indication of their understanding. It may be that your instructions are not clear. We always think we have explained ourselves clearly, but that is not always the case.

6. Give long answers to their questions. You need to communicate using the same level of detail as the other person. If your answers are short and lacking in detail, it appears to this person that you do not know what you are talking about. They will simply start asking for even more detail or giving you even more because they think you don't understand the situation.

7. Summarise what they have said rather than just responding "Yes" or "No." This helps them to feel that they have been listened to and will help to reduce their "waffling."

   ➤ Wrong -"Yes."

   ➤ Correct - "Yes, I think we should replace the old photocopier. I am glad you have looked at seventeen different models and analysed the prices so carefully. I agree that we should go with the Model RTD 1000. It will give us the best deal and meet our needs very well. Thank you for putting in so much effort."

8. Summarise all agreements in writing and obtain the specific agreement to the contents with the individual. Then either send them a hard copy or a confirming email.

9. Help them to see the big picture or overview. Show them where their responsibilities fit in with others' responsibilities using diagrams. They find this hard to do for themselves.

10. Give instructions in step-by-step form.

    > Wrong — "Do a plan for the PDR project."

    > Correct — "Identify the equipment needed for the PDR project."

        × "Phone the manufacturers and find out the cost for each piece of equipment and its lead time."

        × "Find out the deadline required by John Simpson."

11. "Give me the information by Wednesday 19th."

12. Do not get upset about strange misunderstandings. It's not you! This happens because they tend to remember a small detail of a conversation (and sometimes only one or two, not everything they need to remember), whereas most people remember the gist of the whole thing. Listen to what they have to say. Explain what you really meant, take a deep breath and move on.

Theory of Detail-Oriented People

This is a more common set of behaviours than you might think. It seems to come from an extreme orientation to detail but no flexibility or ability to see the big picture.

All the symptoms stem from this lack of flexibility and being stuck in the detail.

1. Imagine a long cardboard tube, the kind you get inside a roll of wrapping paper. Suppose you could only view the world through this tube and you had to find your way from your home to the nearest shop.

2. This is the world of a person who can only see detail. The very small view of the world makes long term planning and prioritising very difficult. It makes seeing the big picture almost impossible.

3. It makes linking separate events together very hard. Understanding the context of situations and actions becomes mainly a matter of chance.

4. Misunderstandings occur easily because this person will remember a very small part of a conversation or home in on one sentence in an email. They will misinterpret it — often by taking it literally — and frequently take offence where none was intended.

5. Once they have a problem to deal with, that is all they can see and it occupies all their thoughts. They can't "see round it" or "get over it" because the scope of their view is so limited. They need help in order to get out of their own way and see beyond the immediate and minute detail.

6. However, once they have gotten past a problem, it is out of their mind and they will be concentrating on the next small area.

7. These people often see themselves as very reliable because, in their small area of focus, they are doing exactly what they think they should be doing. Things outside that are simply not in their consciousness.

Negative People

Easy to spot, hard to stand for very long ... negative people bring everyone down with their attitudes and approach to business and to life. While you likely have had plenty of experiences, which have illuminated the attributes of negative people, here are some very distinctive behaviours to look out for:

1. **The glass is half-empty.** They see all the down sides to everything.

2. **There are problems with everything.** When you come up with a brilliant idea they immediately tell you why it won't work. This is sometimes disguised as "playing devil's advocate" or looking for potential problems. Don't be fooled though ... when everything is a problem, there attitude is exactly that: a problem.

3. **They focus on what they don't have.** These are the kind of people who always tell you what they haven't got, what they can't do and what is wrong with everything.

What to do:

You may be surprised, but the way to get them to be more positive is to be more negative than they are!

1. For example, when they say, "This is awful" you should agree.

   ➢ Correct — You say, "Yes, it's terrible, I don't think we'll be able to make it."

2. If you want to get them to do something, instead of saying

   ➢ Wrong — "This will be great – you'll love it!" Instead, you say:

   ➢ Correct — "This is probably impossible, I don't think we'll be able to do it, we haven't got anyone with the right skills and knowledge..."

   It sounds counter intuitive, but just try it.

Theory of Negative People

1. These people are motivated to move away from pain and things they don't like. They filter out most of the cheerful information that comes in and see only the depressing and upsetting.

2. Often they are so focussed on what they do not want that they find it impossible to identify what they do want. This makes it hard for them to get what they want to rise to the occasion.

3. What really motivates this person to do something is a serious problem or great pain. By telling them something is impossible or dreadful, you provide this motivation.

4. There is evidence that this is due to the right frontal lobes of the brain being more active than the left. People who are generally cheerful tend to show more activation in the left frontal lobes than the right.

5. Recent research seems to indicate that, with practice this can be changed. You'll just have to practice!

Bullies

No one likes a bully. That's going to be a problem for you, as a manager. This can be a big business problem. Bullying behaviour cannot be tolerated in the workplace, and it is very likely that you have encountered it before and can easily spot it. Bullies are pushy, insensitive and self-focussed ... it's not a pretty sight. Here are some specific behaviours to look out for:

1. **A strong focus on their own needs.** These people do not focus on the needs of others. When they act they do not think about the cost, impact or effect on others.

2. **Negative assumptions about others.** These people often refer to others in derogatory terms, which assumes incompetence or deliberate belligerence.

3. **Telling others what to do.** In many situations they will jump to conclusions without gathering facts and tell others what to do, rather than ask.

4. **Exerting control over others against their will.** Phrases like "you must" and "I will not tolerate" are common.

5. **Blaming others for problems and events.** This person does not tend to take responsibility for his or her own actions. It's always someone else's fault. These people are highly adept at finger-pointing.

6. **Opinions are given as facts.** Statements like "This is useless" and "This is rubbish" are used instead of analysis of the situation and facts.

7. **Personal insults** are delivered in front of others. They use phrases like: "You are an idiot." Or "You are stupid."

8. **The victims tend to think there is nothing they can do.** This is probably the most serious problem of all. They speak in terms of what the person who bullies them "does to" them.

> **Bullies are often closet verbal abusers who can come out of the closet with little provocation. Lemon organisations do not tolerate bullies in the workplace.**

Bullies are often closet verbal abusers who can come out of the closet with less provocation than you might think. If you have a bully in your department or on your team, it is very serious indeed, and it needs to stop immediately. It can be difficult, however, so here are tips on what to do if you are managing someone who is bullying others.

1. Gather the facts from the person who feels bullied and others who have witnessed incidents. Identify what has happened on particular occasions. Make notes.

2. Also identify if the bully is able to behave reasonably. Have they done this in the past? Have they ever made requests in a reasonable way, taking others' needs and views into account?

3. Listen to the bully. Ask them about specific incidents. Find out what their perception is. Do your best just to listen and ask questions without being too judgmental. Often these people feel that no one listens to them.

4. Ask them how they think their behaviour is perceived by others. You will probably discover they have no idea how offensive it is. They probably will not even realise they are doing it.

5. Ask them what it is they need to achieve. Help them to identify the real need, rather than the want.

   ➢ Wrong — "I want him to do the report on time the way I say it should be done."

   ➢ Correct — "I need the report to be done by Friday in the same format as the previous ones."

6. Ask them how else they could deal with the situation. If you know they have behaved acceptably in other situations, you know they are capable of it.

7. If there is no evidence of the bully making reasonable requests in the past, it is quite likely they will have no idea of how to behave differently. You will have to give them a way of doing it. For example:

   ➢ Correct — When you need to ask Jane to do something for you here is how I want you to do it. Say: Jane, the PVR

report needs to be ready for Friday morning. Could you do
it for me please? Thank you.

8. Make it very clear that the previous behaviour is not acceptable. Explain
    what will happen if there are further examples of this behaviour.

9. Help the "bully" to feel safe.   People bullying others often feel
    threatened and frightened. Tell the person that you are there to help
    them and ask what support you can give them.

A bully in the office can send productivity into a nosedive, but there are things
you can do to take the bite out of the bully and teach him (or her) to give up
their bullying attitudes and behaviours and become more Lemon-like in
approach.

What to do:

If you are managing someone who is being bullied, here are two concrete steps
you can take to help that person handle the bully's behaviour.

1. They need to stand up to the bully. This is usually easier to do if
    they approach the "bully" rather than waiting for him or her to
    approach them. They need to make clear requests and statements.
    Often physically standing up in the presence of the person doing the
    bullying (rather than sitting down) can make a big difference.

2. Make it clear to the person experiencing the bullying that you are
    supporting them and that you have spoken with the person doing
    the bullying and told them the behaviour is unacceptable. Explain to
    them how you expect the bully to behave in future and that you will
    be checking up on their progress. Make a date to do this. It is
    critical to ensure the person knows that you will not stand for the
    behaviour in your department/team and that you are managing the
    situation.

What to do:

If you are working with someone, or for someone more senior than you are, who uses bullying behaviour towards you:

Think about your own behaviour if you are working with someone who uses bullying behaviour towards you. Make sure that for your next meeting with the person you use the correct approach.

> ➢ Correct — The time and date are at <u>your</u> convenience

> ➢ Correct — You are prepared

> ➢ Correct — You remain standing (to give you more authority)

> ➢ Correct — You ask the questions e.g. "When do you need this report?"

> ➢ Wrong — You do not use the word "Why" (this can be interpreted as a threat)

> ➢ Correct — You breathe deeply and regularly (this helps you to keep calm).

> ➢ Correct — See also how to deal with temper tantrums

> ➢ Correct — You may need some outside help. Make notes of specific incidents and be sure you stick to the facts.

Theory of Bullies

1. Adults often don't realise they are doing this. When you were at school, you probably knew

Bullying is childish behaviour displayed by adults who have never grown up. These behaviours have to be dealt with in the Adult mode.

which children in your class were going to be bullied before it happened. That's because certain behaviours encourage bullying. Other behaviours discourage it.

2. Most children have learned more effective ways of negotiating than bullying by the time they are five or six. A few do not, and carry on using bullying behaviour into adult life. They need to learn more adult behaviours. Bullying is also a symptom of the Monkey Syndrome and wildly inappropriate versions of the Parent mode in managers and the Child mode in direct reports who do not manage.

3. When we deal with bullying behaviour we are dealing with a five year old behaviour coming from a grown up. This is confusing. As a result we treat the person as if they are grown up, which does not work. We need to treat them as we would a five-year old.

4. We need to make them aware of their behaviour and of its effects. Then we need to help them find more effective ways of behaving.

5. Above all, we need to refuse to be intimidated or to allow ourselves to become angry at the treatment. Both are natural responses to bullying, but they only encourage the bully and prolong the pain. Be fully in your Adult consciousness when dealing with a bully. If you do not respond in the Child mode to their

6. Parent approach, you will throw off their game and it will give you an advantage in dealing with the situation.

Temper Tantrums

Watching adults have temper tantrums in a business situation is extremely off-putting and will lose that person a tremendous amount of respect from everyone who witnesses it. It damages the relationships within the workplace more visibly than some of the other bad behaviours because it is so obvious. A person can't have a temper tantrum in a quite way — everyone within earshot will be a witness to this highly inappropriate behaviour. It will forever impair that individual's ability to perform within the group, causing people to view that person as difficult and unpleasant to work with. If he supervises or manages other people, no one will trust him; and certainly if this behaviour is consistently ongoing, it will quickly erode that person's ability to perform their job.

Although it will be pretty obvious, here are behaviours to look out for:

1. **Lack of awareness**. They rarely know they lost their temper, or were shouting. They do not realise the effect it has on others.

2. **A person starts shouting or losing their temper,** often in an unpredictable way — or it may be entirely predictable.

There are ways to approach people having a tantrum that will help pull them back into more adult behaviours. Here's what you can do:

1. Never interrupt while they are ranting.

2. Wait till they have finished what they needed to say, summarise it, using their language and intonation (so make it sound urgent or angry if they did).

3. Ask them "what would you like me to do about it?" (Don't worry — it will not be as bad as you think — often they won't be able to answer).

4. Tell them what you can and can't do and by when.

5. If they start ranting again, simply repeat the process, it will stop after two or three rounds.

Theory of Temper Tantrums

1. We all have tolerance for a range of emotional responses. Once we leave our window of tolerance, we lose control of our behaviour. This is because we lose access to parts of our cerebral cortex.

2. This loss of control reduces our capacity for listening to others and deploying our reasoning skills.

3. The strategy above helps a person to return to an emotional state where they have more access to their mental faculties.

Indecisive People

Indecisiveness isn't as dramatic as the traits of some other difficult personalities, but it can be as much of a drain on productivity. It is a very prevalent trait among the people we have been highlighting as operating in their Child mode. In Child mode, indecisives will fling those Monkeys with surprising frequency and force, because they just can't make up their minds. Often, they can't get either started or finished when facing the responsibilities that come with their jobs.

Behaviours to look out for

1. **Procrastination**. People delay making decisions, initiating a project and taking action.

2. **Frequent changing of mind.** Agreements are made and then changed time and time again.

3. **No decisions** are made at all within their given role and during any special projects to which they may be assigned.

What to do:

1. Find the criteria. You need to help the other person to find out what are their criteria for making the decision. You do this by asking: "What's important about...." Whatever she says she needs is a starting point to helping her set up her own decision-making process. If appropriate, you might like to add your own criteria.

2. Then make the decision. Once you have the criteria, you then use them to help the person make the decision. This is done by weighing any options against the criteria you have identified. Help them get to a decision by asking more questions. The conversation might go like this:

    > ➤ Q. "What's important to you about this date?"

    > ➤ A. "It needs to be before Christmas and on a day the whole team can make."

    > ➤ Q. "What else?"

    > ➤ A. "I guess we will need a day when the board room is available."

    > ➤ Q. "Anything else?"

    > ➤ A. "Oh yes, not a day when we have a rush on in production, so not the month end."

    > ➤ Q. "Is that it?"

    > ➤ A. "Yes."

    After that brief discussion, she will realise everything she needs to decide when and how to set up the meeting.

3. Offer her a series of options (if appropriate) for how she is going to do it. "I could check the diary, ask Graham to do that, or we could look now on the system. What would suit you best?"

4. Go through how she could have arrived at the decision by looking at the results of the research she had pulled together.

   ➢ Correct — "The dates that were available for the team were 4, 15, 19, 21 and 28th. The boardroom is only available for 21st and 28th. The 28th is too near the end of the month, so let's book the 21st."

5. Write the criteria down. If the person changes her mind, remind her of what it was she wanted to achieve and what she said was important.

6. Offer several options. When dealing with this person in general, do not force this person to one solution. This is most unlikely to work. Even being able to offer small amounts of choice will help. However, make sure your criteria are stated clearly:

   ➢ Correct — "I need the report by Friday – would you like to fax it, email it or give me a hard copy?"

In this way you are guiding him toward the results you want, but you are also teaching him to make a decision by giving him three viable options to choose from that will each bring about the end result you desire.

Theory of Indecisive People

1. Making decisions involves a process. Very often people who find it difficult to make decisions are missing a step in that process. That step is identifying their criteria. By helping them to discover what the appropriate criteria are, you will help them to make a decision.

2. Telling people what they must do can often make things worse. If they feel forced down a particular route they will often change their minds later. Therefore, for best results, make sure you always give some element of choice somewhere in your dealings with them.

Most people, either in their personal life or at work, have to deal with difficult people. Their contributions to an organisation can be greatly improved and the number of problems they cause within the organisation can be substantially decreased if the manager takes the time to work with them. It takes finesse and patience, though, and it won't happen over night, so get ready for something of a journey to healthier behaviour for these difficult people.

Key Points Summary

- ◆ Objectives must be **SMART** — **S**pecific, **M**easurable, **A**chievable, **R**ealistic and **T**ime-bounded

- ◆ SMART objectives help to create a line of sight for the employee between their objectives and the direction of the organisation

- ◆ Negative or one dimensional objectives can be neither managed nor measured

- ◆ Avoid non-specific phrases in constructing objectives that lead to woolly objectives ... they can't be measured, so they aren't achievable

- ◆ For most people, four to six objectives will be manageable, keep them focussed and motivated and cover the key aspects of their professional development. Fewer has less meaning and provides little "stretch" incentive. More can be confusing and frustrating.

- ◆ Coaching, done properly, helps the coachee become completely self-aware, self-confident and capable of delivering successful results independently and with enthusiasm

- Achieving one's potential and performing at the highest levels requires a belief in the possibilities, self-confidence, commitment and awareness

- A successful coach holds a belief that the individual has the potential and ability to be successful and has the desire to help the individual tap into that potential and unleash the success within herself.

- Appraisals are part of your management process, not a stand-alone procedure

- Appraisals grade an individual's performance, not the individual

- Give feedback as occasions arise during the year

- Deal with problems promptly during the year

- Make sure you are familiar with the system in your organisation and how it works

- There should be no surprises in the appraisal

- Prepare thoroughly

- Stick to facts, avoid opinions

- Emphasise what the individual has done well and their strengths

- Be clear what they need to do to improve

- Listen to what the other person says

- Make sure the comments on the form are honest and fit with the facts

- Make sure the objectives are clear and measurable

- Feedback is information about an individual's actions and their consequences that helps them to learn

- Feedback should be based on facts, not opinions

- Non-specific praise and negative instructions can reduce a person's performance because it doesn't provide any positive or concrete information on which to act

- The purpose of communication within an organisation is to move people to action

- Communication is about sharing thoughts that create mutual understanding

- A self-aware manager who recognises his own communication style and who also realises that it is important to be able to recognise the style used by others

- Understanding the left brain – right brain context, and the functional differences between the two predominant patterns of behaviour, is the first step in becoming more flexible in your communication style

- "Difficult people" leave chaos in their wake and a wise manager learns to spot and handle them deftly and quickly

- Bullies can do irreparable damage to an organisation and can't be tolerated

Turning Monkeys Into Lemons

A HIGH-PERFORMING ORGANISATION ACHIEVES THROUGH THE LEADERSHIP AND FOLLOWERSHIP OF MOTIVATED, ENGAGED LEMONS

Learnings

Turning Monkeys into Lemons is fundamentally a book about Performance Management. Its central theme is that many mangers and leaders fall into the trap of breeding the Monkey Syndrome rather than growing Lemons. As you've seen, the Monkey Syndrome that is rampantly active within an organisation is destructive and counter-productive. It disables a department or team and renders both the manager and the direct report less than able to produce results, but for different reasons. The manager simply doesn't have any time left after he has wrangled monkeys all day to coach, teach or model successful behaviour. The direct report, by handing over his Monkeys, vacates the learning process and creates his own dis-incentives, thereby continuing to inhabit a stagnant, disempowered existence. The manager turns to Parental behaviour when confronted with lacklustre producers and further disables his team through his own inability to manage properly. **Big Lesson #1:** There will **always** be Monkeys. It's the manager's job to handle only those he is legitimately responsible for, and conscientiously deflect back to the rightful owner any that he is not. He and his employees will be happier and more successful in the long run if he does so.

> **By handing over his Monkeys, the subordinate vacates the learning process and creates his own dis-incentives.**

Growing Lemons, on the other hand, is the metaphor that best illuminates the organisation that is filled with creative, self-confident, self-aware and self-motivated individuals who have learned to observe their own behaviour, edit themselves, seek coaching and strive for objectives that reach outside themselves ... and do so consistently. Lemons objectives are in sync with the needs of their organisation, because they understand why they are there and what they are there to do ... and they have made a conscious choice to continue being there and doing it. They feel fulfilled by the work they do and the environment in which they do it. It is possible for them to achieve this and be this in a non-Lemon organisation through their own internal drive and the fruits of their continuous self-discovery, but successful high-achievers thrive best in Lemon organisations, where they are surrounded by Lemon managers and leaders who model, teach and coach them to new heights. **Big Lesson #2:** Lemons succeed. Lemons live their lives and enjoy doing it. Lemon behaviour can be taught ... and learned!

Managing Performance in Lemon organisations and as a Lemon manager requires a special approach to management responsibilities. Adherence to Adult behaviour patterns and the techniques for coaching and modelling in Adult mode is essential in the development of Lemons, as is supporting their process of self-development and their achievement of focussed professional objectives and objectives which form a tie between the complimentary purposes of the individual and the organisation. When an individual has enough self-knowledge and understanding of what creates fulfilment and a sense of purpose in them, they will be able to choose an organisation with like-minded people, overarching complimentary values, and a business purpose that is synchronised with their drive for achievement. In short, Lemons "find" Lemon organisations — they are drawn to the aura of intellectual energy, creativity and success created by people who are energetic, creative and successful. Lemons can also be nurtured and coached into existence by Lemon managers and leaders, who will be enlightened enough to spot the possibilities inherent in good people with talent, enthusiasm and capability. For high-performing individuals in high-performing organisations there is an undeniable connection between the interests of the company and the interests of the individual coming together to produce often ground-breaking results. Having said that, those high-performing organisations and individuals would be hard pressed to keep the connection without the linkage of the Lemon traits and attributes we have spent so much time exploring in this book.

Cultivating Lemons is very much about making and keeping the enthusiasm and engagement flowing within an environment that celebrates and uplifts those enthusiastic contributors and feeds their need for substance and consistency.

It is also painfully clear that in organisations that have been labelled as living in the Monkey Syndrome, the disconnect often is as palpable as the connection found within and between Lemons and their organisations. Stressed out, harried, careless managers and leaders breed equally stressed out, often low-achieving employees because there is no energy in the departments or teams that are filled with time management and performance issues. Energy and dedication simply does not flow from high absence, low productivity teams, managed and lead by people who are barely keeping their heads above water and spending a lot of time looking for ways to blame their direct reports for their team's lack of success. **Big Lesson #3**: If your people aren't achieving, look in the mirror.

It is my objective in sharing with you these concepts, along with my experiences with individuals, managers and businesses, that you will recognise some of the varied traits we have discussed in yourselves, and that you will be able to either nurture them or change them, depending on which side of the metaphor they fall. The significant point is that none of these issues are written anywhere in concrete. Desire and dedication can change any situation. You will have found a myriad of purposeful steps you can take if you see yourself sinking beneath the Monkey Syndrome. My purpose is not to shame you into it. Rather, my purpose is to present such a compelling alternative through the achievement possibilities of the Lemons in this book that you will want to take the journey for yourself.

Going forward, my wish is that you identify what makes you love the work you do ... or not. Make a list and then compare it with both the stated and the applied mission and vision of your organisation. Then ask yourself these things:

- ◆ Are the things that drive your sense of accomplishment in sync with the actions that make your company a success?

♦ At the end of the day, do you feel you are accomplishing things that give you a sense of fulfilment and pride?

♦ Do you feel successful, and can you see the acknowledgement of your success in the rewards and recognition you receive from your company?

If you can answer "yes" to these questions, then you are where you should be ... you have found an organisation in which you fit, and that meets your needs and promotes in you a sense of self-fulfilment, self-actualisation and "rightness." Now, congratulate yourself, because you may be very unusual indeed. Finally, look at the kind of manager you are. Can you honestly say that you spend your time coaching, training and managing people rather than managing the tasks your people should be doing? Have you any screaming monkeys camped out on your desk or hanging around your shoulders right now? Do you feel you have a team of motivated, challenged and high-achieving contributors, or are you saddled with a lot of people whom you consider "problem employees?" Take an honest look at your organisation and how the people in it operate. Are you proud of their accomplishments and have they contributed to helping you build a successful, well-respected department/division/team? If you see symptoms of the Monkey Syndrome in full swing, you have some work to do. You actually may have some of the wrong people in the right jobs. If so, fix it. Or, you may unconsciously fall back on your "Parent," promoting an order-taking mentality that frustrates your direct report's efforts to do their own jobs. There are many tips and tools in the book to help you identify your own and other's destructive behaviour patterns. All you have to do is to be willing to take a close look at how you operate as a manager and how that impacts your direct reports.

Big Lesson #4: Take care of the management basics ... it is your most important responsibility as a manager and leader of people. Pay close attention to the actions that create a distinction between the manager who is focused on tasks and the one who is focused on people. Dedicate yourself to the discipline of performance management, not because it is in your job description, but because it is a practice that truly gives you the best opportunity to nurture your Lemons and turn those who are caught up in Monkey behaviour into Lemons. Practice performance management on an ongoing basis, with a running dialogue between you and your direct report. Surprises are never a good way to manage performance … not for you and not for your direct reports. If you let them know what you are thinking about their performance and what you want them to do differently, you are very likely to get what you want. And, moreover, expecting senior people to read your mind or "just know" because they are experienced what you need and want from them is the quickest way to mutual failure. On rare occasions you may run across someone who is so in tune with your way of thinking that you feel they can almost read your mind. While that may feel very gratifying, and it is certainly a time-saver, it has a down side: neither one of you is feeding the other new, creative thoughts and ideas. You will have to guard against the possibility that you and your direct report may develop a "yes-man" relationship.

In the final chapter of *Turning Monkeys Into Lemons*, we focused specifically on some of those other basics of managing people and their performance: Objective setting, Coaching Skills, Feedback Skills, Appraisal Skills, Communication and Managing Difficult People. Along with the broader view of performance management, these are the cornerstones of managing an organisation's "human capital." Doing these things right … and in fact, "right" is often not enough, you must actually excel at these skills to move your organisation forward … is what differentiates a soaring, high-performing organisation from one that is earthbound (just making it, or worse). The tips and lessons of this chapter came from my years working with managers in real-life situations, coaching and teaching them how to do the same thing for their people. These techniques work … they are field tested and proven … and my wish is that you are able to turn them to your own advantage, and use them to improve your organisation's performance, your own satisfaction, and your company's success.

The principles, lessons and philosophies found in *Turning Monkeys Into Lemons* can and will, if applied, most certainly help you be a better, more successful manager in many ways. They can also save your organisation a lot of money. **Big Lesson # 5**: Monkeys are expensive! Go back to the Monkey Calculator if you've forgotten how expensive Monkeys are for an organisation. Knowing that you can quantify the impact of the Monkey Syndrome on your organisation can be a shock, but it should certainly be an incentive in itself to start working on identifying the shortcomings of your team, cultivating your high-performing Lemons, and identifying others who have the potential to develop into Lemons. If nothing else, it should certainly make achieving your financial performance objectives easier by reducing the budgetary drain of rampant Monkey behaviour.

Finally, I would say to you that finding the **zest** is fun, it's rewarding and it pays off! Don't let those Monkeys get the best of you. Cultivate some Lemons ... you'll be glad you did!

Lightning Source UK Ltd.
Milton Keynes UK
04 May 2010

153672UK00001B/230/P